# Mother, Can You *Not*?

# Mother, Can You *Not*?

*And You Thought Your Mom Was Nuts . . .*

KATE SIEGEL

CROWN ARCHETYPE
NEW YORK

Published in the United States by Crown Archetype,
an imprint of the Crown Publishing Group,
a division of Penguin Random House LLC, New York.
crownpublishing.com

Crown Archetype and colophon is a registered trademark of
Penguin Random House LLC.

Library of Congress Cataloging-in-Publication Data
Names: Siegel, Kate, author.
Title: Mother, can you not?: and you thought your mom was nuts . . . /
Kate Siegel.
Description: First edition. | New York: Crown Archetype, 2016
Identifiers: LCCN 2016000957 (print) | LCCN 2016004236 (ebook) |
ISBN 9781101907047 (hardback) | ISBN 9781101907054 (tradepaper) |
ISBN 9781101907061 (eBook)
Subjects: LCSH: Mothers and daughters—Humor. | Jewish women—
Humor. | BISAC: HUMOR / Topic / Relationships.
Classification: LCC PN6231.M68 S54 2016 (print) | LCC PN6231.M68
(ebook) | DDC 818/.602080353—dc23
LC record available at http://lccn.loc.gov/2016000957

ISBN 978-1-101-90704-7
eBook ISBN 978-1-101-90706-1

Printed in the United States of America

*Book design by Gretchen Achilles*
*Jacket design by Matt Chase*
*Photograph and illustration credits appear on page 255.*

3 5 7 9 10 8 6 4 2

FIRST EDITION

For Mom and Dad

# Contents

Dear Lawyer Evaluating This Book,

1. I'm sorry.

You probably took this job, vetting manuscripts for Penguin Random House, to read books by important authors like Salman Rushdie and the PRESIDENT OF THE UNITED STATES. You certainly didn't sign up to read about my mother's vagina. So for that, I apologize.

2. I'm so sorry.

As you read these essays, you may be shocked by some of the mortifying situations my mother has gotten herself (and me) into over the years. In an effort to avoid humiliating (and getting sued by) innocent third parties who appear in this book, I have changed names and small details to protect their identities. Hell, I wish *I* could assume a fake name for some of these stories! For instance, I would love to pretend it was my *sister* who was the accomplice to my mother's cat larceny instead of me. Alas, I do not have a sister.

3. I'm so very, very sorry.

That last point in section two brings me to the following elephant in this metaphorical room: my mom has had a few minor brushes with the law! And I've written about some of them in this book! I've done a fair amount of research, as I don't want my mom to go to jail (most of the time), and I believe the statute of limitations has expired on the criminal offenses disclosed in the essays. But of course, you're the one with the law degree, so I'll defer to you!

Truly Sorry,
Kate Siegel

# Mother, Can You *Not*?

3:20 pm

< Messages **Mother** Details

@CrazyJewishMom

Kate I sat next to the nicest young man at Starbucks today. Yale. Lawyer. I showed him your Facebook picture and gave him your number.

Mom you can't keep giving my number out to strangers

YALE

# Introduction

When my mother was twenty-five years old, she moved to Los Angeles to pursue her dream of becoming a television director. She hitched a ride to Hollywood with no idea how to drive, no job, and no place to live (unless you count the floor of a garage in West Hollywood without direct access to plumbing or heat). She was ultimately successful, even nominated for a directing Emmy, but in the early days, she had no money and wrote porn scripts to pay the rent. When asked about that time in her life, she always remembers it proudly: “Oh, honey, it was fabulous! So, I wrote a few pornos? You do what you have to, and it was fun!”

Incidentally, if anyone reading this is in possession of a late ’70s skin flick called *The Bionic Tool,* please email me at crazyjewishmom@gmail.com. My mom doesn’t remember her “porn name,” so the writing credit could either be Kim Friedman or (if I had to guess) her superhero alter ego, "The Castrator."

Given my mother's job history, I suppose I should have anticipated a positive response when I told her about a seemingly crazy idea I had for a project: sharing our intensely personal conversations on the Internet every day.

At this point, I should mention that my mother texts me a lot. Like, *a lot*. Seriously, I counted. She averages 111 text messages a day.

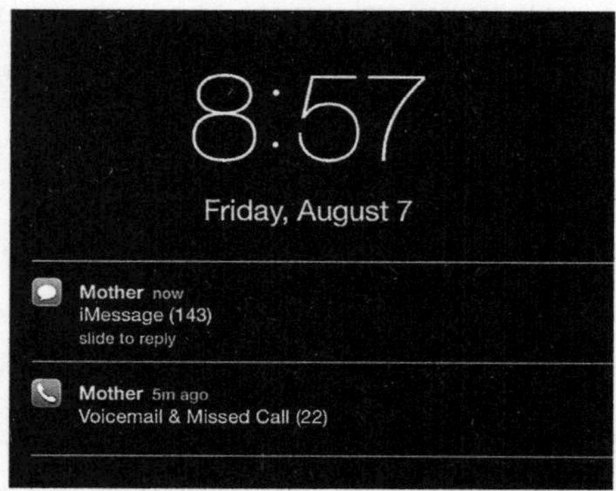


In light of the content of these messages, I had some serious privacy concerns when I thought about sharing them.

OMG. Did u have sex last night??

SO INAPPROPRIATE. Go away

Kate I just read that Rubbers Made in China may have HOLES IN THEM. U NEED MORE SPERM BLOCKAGE

Let's get u a diaphragm NOW.

Mom please stop

But Diaphragms are back in style! They are on fleak!

Her reaction to my idea was: "TRY IT! I mean, I'd prefer you make an app and become a billionaire Mark Zuckerberg with ovaries, but are you kidding me?! What are you afraid of!? Try *something*! You're not getting any younger." With my mother's "encouragement," I began posting screenshots of our conversations on Instagram.

Good morning Spawn. KEGEL ALERT KEGEL ALERT KEGEL ALERT KEGEL ALERT!

Mother, you have to stop doing this. IT'S NOT FUNNY!!!!!

Kate This isn't a joke. If u don't vaginacise every day ur lady bits will explode when u have a baby.

Do u want that to happen? Do your Kegels. Seriously.

I immediately regretted the decision: "OH DEAR GOD, WHAT HAVE I DONE?! HOW AM I EVER GOING TO BE TAKEN SERIOUSLY AFTER PEOPLE KNOW THAT MY MOM TEXTS ME DAILY KEGEL REMINDERS AND HAS A LOT TO SAY ABOUT DILDOS AND MY VAGINA IN GENERAL?" Sharing my personal life so publicly was a major adjustment, and for the first few weeks, I wanted to hide in my apartment. Was my boss's boss's boss's boss just staring at me because of last night's vagina post? *Probably not, as he didn't know my name.* Was my dry cleaner smirking about the soy sauce stain on my blazer, or because he read this afternoon's conversation about waxing my boyfriend's pubic hair?

After a few months of getting accustomed to the fact that a wealth of information about my vaginal canal was publicly available, I just leaned in to all the oversharing. Hey, if my dental hygienist is already well versed in my mother's anal bead curiosity, why not strangers in Iowa? So, when an editor named Morgan Shanahan reached out about writing an article on @CrazyJewishMom for BuzzFeed, I thought *why the hell not?*

That weekend, my boyfriend and I were visiting my parents' house, and we went to lunch at a little hole-in-the-wall Vietnamese restaurant my dad and I love. Unfortunately, the restaurant is in the back of an Asian supermarket that smells like the inside of a whale's rectum. My mother was grimacing as we sat down.

"Uch, this place is disgusting." She turned to my father. "Hey, Michael, tomorrow do you want to take me to dinner in a Porta Potty? I saw a really nice one at a construction site on the way here."

I pulled out my phone to check Instagram, leaving my father to fend for himself. Thousands of new followers flashed onto my screen. I refreshed my feed again, one hundred more in less than a second! "Jon! Look!" I grabbed my boyfriend's arm.

"Kate, turn that off." My mom glared at me.

"No wait." She reached for my phone, but I put a hand up. "Seriously hang on, something crazy is happening." I refreshed BuzzFeed for the fiftieth time that day, and the interview was finally live!

"Oh my god!" Thousands of new followers were pouring in, and my heart started fluttering. "Oh my Go—I—I—I have to throw up!" Perhaps the orca butthole contributed, but I jumped up from the table, ran to the bathroom, and puked up the entire contents of my stomach and possibly some of my small intestine.

"You see, Michael?" My mom smacked my dad on the shoulder as I walked back toward the table. "You take us to places like this and we all get food poisoning and die." Note: We hadn't eaten yet. My dad and Jon looked at me with concern.

"I'm fine, I'm fine. They did an article about the Instagram account on BuzzFeed. I think it's going viral!"

"What's Buzz Freed?" My dad tilted his head quizzically.

"You mean, the blog?" My mother pulled sanitizing wipes from her purse. "So that's good, right? What's with all the vomit drama?" Yes, she called the Instagram account a "blog" for the first five months. Now she usually refers to it as "Kate's Instagram App," and in light of my recent promotion to CEO of Instagram, I'd like my stock options now, please.

"Give me your phone, Mom." I smiled. "I need to sign you up for an Instagram account, so you can see the text messages I share."

"What do I need to look at them for?" She picked up a chopstick with disgust and began cleaning it with a Handi-Wipe. "*I'm* the one who sends them to you. If I want to look at them, I'll look at my text messages."

"Yes, but don't you want to follow? What if I post a conversation you don't like?"

"Honey, if I say it to you, I mean it. I give great advice! So, let everyone see it; it'll help people. And besides, I really don't care what people think. This is me."

In a week, @CrazyJewishMom had gone fully viral. The Instagram account went from having about 13,000 followers to 300,000, all watching and waiting to see what hilarious new adventure my mom and I would get into next.

OMG GET DOWN HERE! THOR GOT THE TURKEY!! HE'S HUMPING IT AND SNARLING AT EVERYONE!!!

My baby's in love!

MOM NOT FUNNY! What are we going to do?? We have people to feed!

Oh relax, we'll just wash it off and cook it. no one will know.

MOM WHERE THE HELL ARE YOU!?! The turkey needs to cook for like 5 hours!!!

Calm down. First place had no organic free range pasture fed antibiotic/hormone free birds. Still looking.

Mom! You're not going to find organic ON THANKSGIVING DAY! Just get any turkey!

U'll thank me when u don't sprout a third boob from the hormones.

• • • • • • • • • • • • • • • • • • • • • • • • • • • • • • • • • • • •

However, my mother was *involved* long before the advent of the text message or Instagram. When asked about her parenting style directly, her response is usually: "Helicopter Mom? Please! I'm a Drone Mom!"

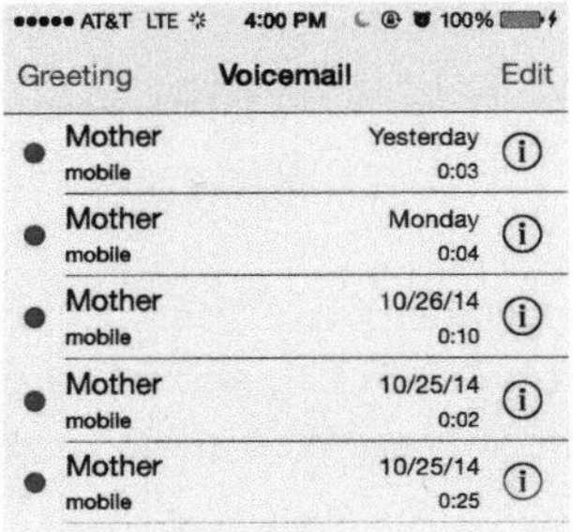

●●●●● AT&T LTE 4:00 PM 100%

Greeting **Voicemail** Edit

| | | |
|---|---|---|
| ● | Mother<br>mobile | Yesterday<br>0:03 |
| ● | Mother<br>mobile | Monday<br>0:04 |
| ● | Mother<br>mobile | 10/26/14<br>0:10 |
| ● | Mother<br>mobile | 10/25/14<br>0:02 |
| ● | Mother<br>mobile | 10/25/14<br>0:25 |

Her obsession with my well-being and future truly began when I was in utero. She refused to wear deodorant for a full nine months—"the aluminum!"—and she read Shakespeare to "fetus me" for one hour each day when I was in her womb.

The best way I can describe her shenanigans while I was growing up is that it was like living in an episode of *I Love Lucy*. She was Lucy, and I was constantly roped in as Ethel, her unwitting accomplice.

• • • • • • • • • • • • • • • • • • • • • • • • • • • • • • • • • • •

YOU KNOW THINGS
ARE BAD
WHEN YOUR HUSBAND
FINDS THE NEW
CLOTHES YOU SNUCK
IN FROM THE CAR
LAST NIGHT

**OMG. Look at this meme. This is your life in a nutshell.**

**Please, that's amateur hour. The trick is to put it in a Whole Foods bag and pretend ur heading for the kitchen, then sneak upstairs**

(I keep stacks of empty bags in my car.) Or sometimes I just put it in a dry cleaning bag and hang it all right in our closet. cut the tags off when he's sleeping.

The mother-daughter relationship is a complex one though. As a daughter, you have to respect the fact that this woman grew you inside of her for nine months and then squeezed your watermelon-sized ass out of a small, sensitive hole. A hole that up to the point only ever experienced kielbasa- (if she's a lucky lady/owns a vibrator, maybe bratwurst-) sized objects passing through. Add to that the unconditional love, diaper changing, and years of vile bodily fluid clean-up duty, and there's a lot to be grateful for.

But watermelons and vaginas aside, there is no one else on the planet who knows where all your emotional land mines are buried, and exactly how to get away with tripping them. For instance, my mother will sometimes ask me this: "Kate, whatever happened to that adorable green skirt? You still have it, don't you? It looks so good on you!" Seems innocuous, right? So when I detonate with "SHUT UP, MOM! I DON'T NEED THIS RIGHT NOW, OKAY? LEAVE ME ALONE!!!!" it's confusing for the casual observer. She always responds to my explosion with feigned bewilderment: "What? All I did was ask about that skirt you love! What's the issue?"

The Issue(s):

1. The skirt in question was purchased in 2003 and last fit me when I was a sophomore in high school.
2. Said skirt is not missing! It is hanging in my mother's closet, because when she's not affecting faux confusion about my atomic green-skirt response, she's saying: "Someday it might fit you again."

When my mother says, "Kate, whatever happened to that adorable green skirt?" I hear, *Kate, you're fat. Get to the gym, lard-o,* and she knows it. Likewise, since I know that my mom is sensitive about her (large) breasts, when I say, "Mom, why don't you just go to Victoria's Secret? You love their bras!" I know she hears, *HAH HAH! Victoria's Secret doesn't make straps big enough to restrain those industrial-grade milk jugs!*

When you have a close relationship with your mother, you develop a kind of secret language that only you and she understand. It's a language that can imbue an otherwise boring object with enough surreptitious, charged meaning to provoke a blood-boiling rampage of repressed rage with a single word. For instance, *skirt*.

Maybe you should freeze your eggs. A lot of single Young Hollywood is doing that. And the guys are freezing their sperm. I guess the current thought is that young eggs and sperm are better. It's like insurance for better babies in case u marry late.

What makes you think I'm going to marry late?

Honey, it's already late.

The secret language isn't only used for sly insults though—it's the same language that allows me to glance at my mother across the table and know we're both trying to figure out if the couple next to us is a father-daughter or sugar daddy–sugar baby situation.

It's also the language that enables me to wordlessly express, *OH DEAR GOD, this food is disgusting! How are we going to get out of here without eating anything and insulting our new neighbor? OH NO! I MIGHT PUKE!* And for her to silently respond: *It's fine, they have a dog. Follow my lead, and just sneak food under the table little by little.* Incidentally, I should have been able to figure that one out on my own, as the dog in question was morbidly obese.

It's the same language that allows us to scream at each other about a stupid green skirt like Mel Gibson yelling at a sea of rabbis, but to still know that if push came to shove, we'd jump in front of a moving train or even give up our Spanx if it meant helping each other.

This language ultimately speaks to how close we are, because that level of innate understanding cannot exist without a mutual, unconditional love. That said, I still sometimes want to punch her in the ovary.

Love you mom, thanks for being amazing!

Are u in trouble? Is this code?

No I'm fine

Prove it's u and not a kidnapper.
What's my real hair color?

Literally no idea. Never seen it

Ok hi Spawn. Love u too.

11:34 pm

< Messages **Mother** Details

@CrazyJewishMom

Kate can send me that collage from that photo shoot for ur book cover to post on my Facebook

How do I post this on Facebook?

# It's Kate Elinore Friedman-Siegel, Bitch

Here are a few bullet points from my mother's highly detailed vision of how my life should look:

- **Career:** Rich entertainment attorney with a degree from Harvard Law.
- **Procreation:** Two to four "grandspawn" to leave in her care, freeing me up to HAVE IT ALL! (She's fine with a sperm donor.)
- **Love:** Marry Mark Zuckerberg or Oprah Winfrey.

Judging by this, I'm a huge disappointment with my creative writing aspirations, empty womb, and failure to even meet, let alone marry, Mark or Oprah. Fortunately, my mother recognizes that her meticulously constructed idea of my ideal life is not necessarily what *I* want or even biologically realistic. For instance, while I'm sure Oprah Winfrey is a lovely woman, I have never looked at a clitoris and thought, *Yep. This is for me.*

Like all good parents, my mother ultimately supports *my* dreams. Unlike most parents, she will do everything short of murdering someone to make sure they come true. And, honestly? Capital offenses might be on the table, given the right circumstance. If you come out of Kim Friedman's uterus, you'd better be absolutely positive that whatever dream you share with her is something you actually want.

When I was a teenager, what I wanted was to be a pop star. On reflection, pop stardom was probably not a good fit for someone whose idea of a good time was attending AP English class and writing *Law & Order: SVU* fan fiction. Nonetheless, I penned and recorded two (truly terrible) songs on my computer, and I was convinced I would be the next Britney Spears. An actual lyric I wrote: "If I was the sun, you would be the moon." Subjunctive grammatical error aside, I think we can all agree that this was some pretty groundbreaking songwriting.

Thank God YouTube hadn't taken off yet, because I most definitely would have uploaded those shameful songs to the Internet. Just think, I could have been the first Rebecca "Friday" Black! Though my song probably would have been called "Monday" and celebrated the *end* of the weekend and my excitement about going to AP US History class. (Because *all* the greatest pop songs are inspired by Franco-American relations in the post–WWII era.)

So yeah, my pop-star fantasy was a fairly aggressive delusion. Though I could definitely sing the crap out of a show tune, I couldn't really read music, and I danced like a newborn calf trying to stand for the first time. My signature move was "The Sprinkler," choreography that can literally be done while seated, but I wasn't about to let a pesky little thing like lack of talent get in my way! Neither was my mother, so Project Pop Star was born . . .

Two weeks into my "recording career," I came home

from school one night and found my mom in the living room, dancing around with enthusiasm.

"You are not going to believe what I pulled off."

"I mean, are you going to tell me?" Teenage sass for days!

She rolled her eyes, too thrilled to be annoyed with me. "I just got off the phone with *Atticus Clark-Williamson.*" She paused dramatically and waited for me to hug her or at least well up with tears of sweet gratitude.

". . . Okay, who's that?"

She threw her hands up in the air. "Honestly, Kate, you say you want to be a musician, and you know nothing about the recording industry! Atticus is *the* rock star photographer to the gods!" *Not true.* "My friend Amy told me that he's photographed everyone! Paul McCartney, Christina Aguilera, Bruce Springsteen! AND he has friends at all the major record labels." *Very not true.* "And you're not going to believe this. He's agreed to do a photo shoot for you this weekend for a fraction of his usual rate!" *This part, sadly, was true.*

"This could be it, Kate! If he likes your music and your look . . . he knows EVERYONE! This is your shot!"

While Atticus Clark-Williamson (actual name: Jerry Fleischman) was in fact a professional photographer, a more realistic résumé might have read: "Once *assisted* a 'rock-star photographer to the gods' on one photo shoot where Lindsay Lohan was supposed to show up but then didn't, because she had been hospitalized for 'exhaustion.' "

"Wait, a photo shoot? For what?"

"For your demo cover!"

"But I don't even have a real demo yet. I still need more songs . . ."

That didn't seem to concern her. My mother and Atticus had already planned an elaborate shoot in downtown Los Angeles. "It's going to be fabulous. Atticus is right . . . he's so right! You need a look that will stand out from all the bubblegum crap that's out there now. He's going to get this gritty, edgy, dangerous downtown-looking vibe. I'm so excited."

Things that are wrong with this idea:

1. My songs were about as edgy as a lemonade stand in a gated suburban community. And frankly, that's what I was going for. I wanted to be Britney Spears, not Courtney Love.
2. At that time, parts of downtown Los Angeles were extremely dangerous.

That said, what teenage girl doesn't want to spend a glamorous day prancing around in front of a camera? I gladly went with it. I imagined wind machines and makeup artists touching up my lipstick between pictures: "Kate, you're a natural! Kate, you're gorgeous! Move over, Beyoncé, here comes Kate Elinore Friedman-Siegel!"

When photo-shoot day arrived, my mother woke me with a remarkable amount of enthusiasm for 6 a.m. "Get up! Get up! Get up! It's rock star girl diva day!" Catching her excitement, I threw off my duvet cover and "Sprinkler'd" over to the chair where she had laid out the final four outfits for the photo shoot.

"I really think I nailed the *DANGER* look, Kate, don't you?"

One of the outfits included a Juicy Couture zip-up tracksuit. So no. No, she had not nailed the danger look. We fussed with my hair and makeup, and by the time we left the house, I was feeling good, like Brad Pitt Third Wife Material good.

We met the photographer in a Dunkin' Donuts parking lot, right off the I-10 freeway. He was wearing carefully ripped jeans, a leather vest with no shirt, and beaded bracelets on both arms. He leaned against his vintage Ford Bronco, posing. His hair was artfully swept to one side with enough product to preserve his look in the event of a nuclear blast.

"Oh, there he is! Michael, pull over!" My dad, who had agreed to chauffeur us around all day, tucked the car into the spot next to the Bronco.

My mother leapt out of the car, arms wide. "Atticus! So fabulous to meet you! We're so excited about today."

"Cool. Where's Kate?"

"SPAWN! Get out here!" She waved at me to hurry, and I opened the back door of my dad's car, tottering out on the highest heels I had ever worn. Atticus immediately started snapping photos of me with the Nikon camera dangling from his right hand.

"Um, hi. I'm Kate . . . oh shoot, are you starting? I wasn't ready." I've always wanted to see how those first photos came out—I still had several of my mother's hot-pink rollers in my hair, so I'm sure they were excellent.

"Do you want art or do you want Britney Spears?" I mean, I definitely wanted to be Britney Spears, but it seemed like that wasn't the response Atticus was looking for.

"Oh no, it's just that I didn't realize we were going already. I wasn't ready, so I didn't smile or pose or anything."

"Art can't be posed. I want you raw. I want to feel your emotion!"

"In front of Dunkin' Donuts?"

Atticus sighed. I clearly didn't *get it*. "Listen, let's just go to the first location. I'm already exhausted. I was up all night shooting at the Roxy." He moved toward the door of his truck. "You guys follow in your car."

My mother and I got back into the Volvo with my dad, and she started in on me: "Kate, enough with the attitude. If he tells you to do something, you do it! Did you not hear that?! He was shooting at the *Roxy*!! You need to impress him!" She was drunk on Atticus's Kool-Aid.

"I just didn't know we were starting! I'm sorry! I'll do whatever he wants when we get there!"

My dad followed as Atticus weaved through traffic for fifteen minutes and finally turned onto a narrow, deserted alley in downtown LA. Our caravan pulled up next to an abandoned pickup truck that was decaying against a backdrop of empty warehouses on one side and crumbling apartment buildings on the other. As my dad parked behind Atticus's car, I turned to my mother.

"Wait . . . here?! *This* is the location?"

"Oh relax, you're fine. I have my pepper spray." She hopped out of the car to stand next to Atticus, who was already pretentiously framing the shot with his hands. Atticus pried open the front door of the discarded truck. He didn't even look at me.

"You. In the truck. Now."

I paused, staring at the rusted heap of metal. There

were plants growing on the dashboard and a few shards of broken glass from the shattered windshield in the front seat. *WHERE WERE THE WIND MACHINES? THE MAKEUP ARTISTS?! Hell, I'd have settled for a little Febreze at that point.* I glanced up at my mom.

"Um, *in* the truck? It looks kind of dangerous, and it's all rusty . . ." Atticus gave me a look with more disdain than I imagined possible for a human face.

"Is this going to be a problem? I don't know, I've shot with top models, tons of stars, in far worse places than this."

"You have your tetanus shot—get in there!" My mother glared at me, wiping shards of glass to the floor.

I quickly checked the backseat for dead bodies and then obeyed, carefully avoiding the broken glass, as my mom raved about my music to Atticus.

"It really is amazing, her songwriting. You know, it's too funny, we happen to have a CD with a couple of her songs in the car with us! They're very rough, of course. She just recorded them on her laptop, but you can really hear the raw talent."

"I need silence while I'm working." Atticus held up

a hand. My mother nodded, and whispered, "Perhaps later!"

He started snapping photos of me as I sat awkwardly in the truck, trying to avoid any number of the biohazards surrounding me.

"No. Don't smile. No! Why are you looking at the camera? FEEL YOUR SURROUNDINGS!" I gave a small eye roll, and my mother shot me a look that would have terrified Ted Bundy. Atticus threw up his hands in frustration.

"No, no, this just isn't working. Look at her! She's posing!"

First, I was under the impression that posing is what a person was meant to do in front of a camera. Ironically though, I was not posing at all! I was contorting my body in whatever position seemed least likely to result in a shard of glass severing a major artery. My mother jumped in, trying to salvage the situation.

"Well, maybe we should try some pictures in the alley, with a little movement. I know Kate is much more natural when she's walking . . . and dancing." *Oh dear God, don't make me dance. Something told me Atticus wouldn't appreciate watching me get jiggy with it.* He waved a dismissive arm, signaling that we should try it. "You know what? Let's put on one of Kate's songs, so she can have a little mood music."

"Fine, let's try *something.*" Atticus shrugged.

"Michael! Turn on the CD player! Loud!" my mom shouted over her shoulder to my father, who was sitting in the car reading an old issue of *Boat Trader.*

And so there we were, in the middle of an alley in the most dangerous part of downtown Los Angeles, blasting my terrible pop songs at an earsplitting volume. My mother was staring intently at Atticus, trying to gauge his reaction to my music, as he snapped photos.

"Keep walking . . . now turn away from the camera and walk back. Come on! My God, stop posing! Pretend we're in a fantasy . . . what's your fantasy?" By that point, the only thing I was fantasizing about was punching him in the nuts.

"WEAOOOOOOOAAAAAAAAAHW!"

A deafening, guttural cry drowned out the sound of the angsty-teen beats blaring out of my dad's car.

I reeled back and stumbled onto a cardboard box. As it turned out, that cardboard box was home to a very angry-looking homeless person. I turned and came face-to-face with a shirtless, potbellied man, layers of grime smeared across his pale skin and dreadlocks matting his head. There were well-worn track marks on his arms and an unfocused, furious look in his eyes. Apparently he wasn't a fan of my music. I staggered back, tripping on cans and other refuse in the alley. *You know, like Taylor Swift does on her photo shoots.*

Meanwhile, Atticus was furiously snapping frame after frame of my terror. My pop song with the lyrics "Stop! Hold on! Chill out! Relax! You need to understand that life's a pain in the a-ass!" tangled with the homeless man's raucous bleating. Atticus smiled from behind the camera as I ran.

"Yes! Yes! This is IT! This is what we need. I feel your fear!"

I stumbled a safe distance away, and our new friend was standing motionless, but squawking "WEA-OOOOOOO-AAAAAAAAAHW" every few seconds.

I turned back toward my parents' car; my mom had

already rushed to my side, just out of Atticus's shot, pepper spray in her hand at the ready.

"You're doing great, honey." Atticus was smiling for the first time, and the danger was not imminent, so my mother was not about to mess with that.

Then the homeless man, still bleating, looked directly at me, threw down his pants, and started vigorously masturbating to the beat of my pop song: "No ma-tter what—you try—to do-o-o! Life comes along and makes a fool outta you!"

Now, I should take a moment to point out that this was the first erect penis I had ever seen. Not exactly how I had imagined it happening, or frankly how I pictured it would look. At the time, my fantasy about how this moment would play out involved my history study partner throwing off his glasses and having his way with me on a pile of abandoned Cold War flash cards. So this was different.

At that point, even Atticus's mouth dropped open, and he lowered the camera to stare. My mother stepped between me and the homeless man, raising the pepper spray. She glanced back toward our dumbfounded photographer.

"What're you, crazy!? Atticus, get in there and shoot! She looks gorgeous!"

He was frozen, but the residents of the building that faced the alley were accustomed to this man's behavior. Before Atticus could snap another photo, a torrent of water was hurled over all of us from a balcony above. Soaking wet, I looked up to find a woman holding a bright green bucket.

"Oh shit! I didn't see y'all down there!" I glanced nervously over at the homeless man. "Ah, don't worry about old Vic, he's harmless, just gotta hose him down when he gets riled up!" She noticed he wasn't wearing pants and was still viciously masturbating. "Well, shit. Looks like he's got a sweet tooth for you, little girl!" She laughed and then looked over at my dad's car. "And can you turn off that terrible music!? Lord!"

7:15 pm

< Messages **Mother** Details

@CrazyJewishMom

Omfg I just got home and there were two roaches IN MY SINK. I hate everything. Exterminator coming tommw at 10. Blerghh can u let him in?

**NO EXTERMINATOR! Why don't u just drink a gallon of cancer milk from Chernobyl?? Bug juice fries your ovaries and god forbid makes u sterile. Just move. No more mason jars, no more DIY. Brooklyn is over.**

**Meanwhile I will look for an organic cockroach killer.**

# Because Cancer

*"Even if it might be true, why take the chance?"*

—KIM FRIEDMAN,

arguing with my boyfriend at our dining room table while I write this story because, goddamn it, her grandchildren are not going to grow a third limb from the cancer-causing hypothetical power lines outside our hypothetical children's hypothetical bedroom

There has not been a single day in my entire life when my mother has failed to warn me about the danger of getting cancer. Insecticides, contaminated tap water, formaldehyde insulation, lead paint . . . danger at every turn!

The fears all stem from the passing of my mother's aunt Kate, the woman I was named after. My mom cared for Kate in the final months of her battle with cancer. My parents even had their wedding in her hospital room when the doctors decided Kate was too weak to leave her bed, and the experience changed my mother.

How? She became a textbook hypochondriac. If my dad has gas, it's colonoscopy time. If I have a headache, clearly it's a brain tumor. Over the years, anything she could do to limit our exposure to carcinogens, she did.

"You want Lunchables?! LUNCHABLES?! I read a study in the *Harvard Journal of Medicine* about the proven link between preservatives and nitrates and cancer. That crap is loaded with disgusting chemicals that can make a person grow a third eye! If you so much as say the word *Lunchables* to me again, you're grounded until you're thirty!"

At that point, I was six, so "no" probably would have sufficed.

My mom is quite creative. She sees cancer in places that no one else can—even cancer-research scientists.

You know those night-vision goggles that let people see things in the dark? It's like that, but instead of seeing objects at night, my mother sees potential carcinogens everywhere, all the time.

Living in smoggy Los Angeles only exacerbated my mom's hyper-anxiety. On slightly hazy days, she would force me to wear a face mask whenever I wanted to take our dogs out for a walk. If she decreed that there was too much pollution in the atmosphere during the school week, I wasn't allowed to play outside during recess. Medical-grade hospital masks be damned!

Mind you, my mother didn't get her smog alerts from the news or an atmospheric scientist. She just eyeballed the sky every day, and if it looked particularly cancer-y to her, I was stuck inside with my scratch-and sniff stickers.

However, the absolute worst thing for my mother's "cancer is everywhere" worldview was her discovery of electromagnetic radiation. One fateful night in the early '90s, a particularly compelling 3 a.m. infomercial convinced her that electromagnetic radiation waves were:

a. Everywhere.
b. Going to give us all cancer (if they hadn't already).
c. Definitely going to kill her only child.

My moms obsessive fear of all things carcinogenic finally met its neurotic enabler: the electromagnetic radiation field detector (EMF meter, for those in the know).

She ordered two, and these five-pound clunky devices became my mother's most trusted advisors. She took them everywhere with us. If we needed milk, the EMF meter would decide if we were allowed to go into the grocery store and get it. If Becky was having a sleepover, I could go, but if it was at Emily's electromagnetic radiation wave, cancer-riddled excuse for a house, I was out of luck.

When it came time for me to take computer class in elementary school, my mother made me use a special anti-cancer screen protector she bought on HSN. You know, like all the cool third graders do.

When cellphones became a thing, my mother immediately jumped on the "headset cancer avoidance" bandwagon. To this day, if I hold a cellphone against my ear, she either scr[illegible] me or (if it's a business call) waves her li[illegible]til I put the phone on speaker.

Inciden[illegible] phone while my [illegible] a 99 per[illegible] vers[illegible]

U[illegible]

A gift for you

Mom!! Happy Mother's Day!! We hope that you enjoy this book, we follow this mother/daughter duo on Instagram and they are hilarious! They love each other and we love each other! xoxo! Love, Your Girls the John Thomas Dye School (JTD) while I was in utero. In her mind, if I got into JTD, I was a shoo-in for the presidential nom in 2032 (I'm coming for you, Chelsea Clinton). If I did not get in, I'd end up being a lunch-shift stripper. But what if JTD had cancer-y EMF readings? Would she protect me from the radiation or throw me into the White House–bound microwave?

Making sure the school passed her comprehensive "Kate's probably not going to die here" battery of tests became her top priority. Okay, no problem, right? She'd just throw an EMF meter in her bag, head over to John Thomas Dye, and take all the necessary measurements? No. Her thought process: "No way. A teacher might see me and tell the head of the school that I'm a neurotic helicopter parent, always lurking around the campus!"

So, the truth.

The task fell to her intern, Paul, an eager Harvard student who traveled to LA on his summer break to work with my mother on the set of *Star Trek*. I'm sure he imagined coming out to Los Angeles, working with a real Hollywood director, and learning the ropes of show business on the iconic TV show. Instead, he was stuck ferreting out potential carcinogens at elementary schools around Los Angeles for his boss's four-year-old daughter.

At this point, I think it's important to really consider what she was asking her intern to do. She wanted this *adult man* to haul a clunky, bizarre-looking contraption onto the grounds of a school with young children at play and get EMF readings everywhere from the classrooms to the bathrooms.

When Paul nervously raised the pedophile concern to my mother, she told him, "Figure it out. Oh, and don't go on a weekend. I need the readings when the lights are on and the school is in business. If you get caught, never, ever mention my name. Then Kate will never get in!"

I sometimes imagine Paul serving hard time for a crime he didn't commit, defending my spot at the John Thomas Dye School with his freedom.

It never went that far though, because clever Paul ended up faking a flower delivery, concealing the EMF meter in a bouquet of roses to avoid suspicion (and arrest). He even figured out which teacher was single to make his cover story plausible while he walked around the campus, surreptitiously recording EMF readings.

I've always wondered how his story played: "What is an adult man like me doing in the stall of the first grade class girls' bathroom? Why I'm looking for Ms. Ballard's room, of course. As you can clearly see, I've got these flowers and a card addressed to her. Maybe she had a big date? Maybe it went well? But who am I to say? I'm just the flower delivery guy." Proceed!

The John Thomas Dye School passed the test, and I spent five happy, radiation-free years there. And Paul didn't even have to register as a sex offender!

These days my mother's carcinogenic fixation has shifted from obsessively collecting EMF readings to installing a water filtration system under our sink, because the plastic water bottles of my childhood have turned on her in a BPA-laden, cancer-causing frenzy of betrayal. Though she has moved on to fancier, more glamorous carcinogenic threats, my mom will never give up her first love: the EMF meter.

As the saying goes, you never forget your first neurosis.

4:50 pm

< Messages **Mother** Details

@CrazyJewishMom

Just read an article on AOL. The older the sperm, the harder it is to make babies. Lower sperm count.

And you're telling me this because?

NEWSFLASH HONEY, ur boyfriend's no spring chicken. U must freeze his sperm immediately in case he ever pops the question

Please stop talking about my boyfriend's sperm

# Green Eggs and Sperm

Sex is a subject about which my mother has always been very open. With me. With my friends. With my boyfriends. With my elderly Jewish relatives from the old country. Of course, that last example was at the height of her hairy-armpitted sexual-lib phase. At this point, she probably wouldn't think it appropriate to proudly slam her diaphragm and spermicidal gel down on a Seder table and scream at Bubby Klein about birth control pills for men. *Probably.*

I was a pretty epic nerd growing up, so there wasn't really much breaking sex news on my end, unless you consider elaborate fantasies about the Backstreet Boys ripping off my overalls and making tender love to me on the set of Nickelodeon's *Legends of the Hidden Temple* newsworthy. That didn't stop my mother, though! One of the phrases I heard most often growing up was the old standby "Just remember what Grandmom always said: 'Men think with their penises!'"

This candor about sex began when I was almost nine years old, and my mom decided she needed to teach me the facts of life. During the summer before third grade, she let me go to a day camp with my friends in Malibu. As school began in the fall, letters were sent out to all the camp parents, confirming rumors that a teen counselor had molested a young girl that summer. The moment my mom opened that note, she saw red: *TELL KATE EVERYTHING ABOUT SEX, CONSENT, AND KICKING MEN IN THE BALLS RIGHT NOW! GO! GO! GO!*

In third grade, my understanding of reproduction was that when two people fell in love, a baby immediately popped up in the woman's stomach. Then a screaming infant appeared in a bassinet after a few months of eating all her food and kicking her in the ribs. I worried that the moment I touched a boy, a fetus might implant itself in my belly and eat all my Skittles, so I avoided the opposite sex altogether. Just to be safe. *Oh really, Kevin? You want to hold my hand? Well, I want to go to college and establish my career.*

It was a lazy Sunday morning when my mother yelled across the house and told me to get my butt in her room. I hopped into her bed, and she greeted me with a tender "Is that cream cheese on your chin??" I nodded. "Goddamn it, Michael! Kate, you can't let your father feed you that crap. He bought the nonorganic kind again—it's riddled with hormones and chemicals! That's how you get cancer." I sat silently, waiting for Hurricane Neurosis to pass.

"So, there's something I want to talk to you about." My stomach tightened as she pulled out a book from her bedside table with an illustration of a family holding a baby on the cover. The title was something straightforward enough like *Where Do Babies Come From?* Looking back, I've always felt it was a real missed opportunity for some innovative stork puns: *Stick a Stork in Me, I'm Done . . . Believing That Babies Come from Heaven!; Who Needs a Stork? Let's Fork!;* and so on.

"Do you know where babies come from?" My mom opened the book.

"Duh, you told me this already. When a man and a woman fall in love, a baby starts growing in the lady."

"Well, there's a little more to it than that." She proceeded to walk me through twenty mortifying pages about reproduction. The book had a lot of Dr. Seuss-esque illustrations, and it included the phrase "This fits here!"

I remember screaming, "WHAT?! That is DISGUSTING!" Then I shouted across the house to my father and made him join in on the fun. When he opened the door, I shoved in his face a page depicting a cheerful pink man mounting a fuchsia woman. Did I mention the pearl-white sperm seeds shooting out of the pink man's cartoon penis? Well, those were there too.

"Dad, do you know about this?!"

"I . . . well . . . uh—"

"Oh my God!!! I am NEVER EVER EVER EVER EVER EVER EVER EVER EVER EVER EVER doing that!" I threw the book on the bed and whirled back around to my father. "Ewwwww, does that mean you peed in Mom to get me?!"

"Well, uh, not exactly." My dad looked down at his shoes.

"How does that even work? Do you move around!?" I conducted an unbridled, Guantánamo-like interrogation, referencing the diagrams that displayed colorful stick figures having sex in every position under the sun. It was the *Kama Seusstra*.

My parents answered all my questions patiently, and then I asked this: "Well, which position did you guys use to make me?" So "the talk" was going well for my parents!

I vividly remember my mother ending the conversation with a firm warning: "Katie, the other kids at school may not know about the facts of life yet, so you can't tell any of your friends about this." I nodded. She grasped my shoulders and forced me to meet her eyes. "Kate, I'm serious. This is really important. You cannot tell anyone. Other parents may not want their kids to know yet, and it's up to them to tell their children. Not you."

Naturally, the next day I woke up, went to school, and wanted to shout the facts of life from the rooftops! Every time I was tempted to tell someone, my mother's warning rang in my ears, but the Cat in the Hat would not stop humping the Grinch in my daydreams. During gym, a particularly explicit version of *Green Eggs and Ham* was playing on repeat in my head, and I squeezed my eyes shut. My friend Ashley noticed my distress and touched my arm.

"Kate, are you okay? What's wrong?"

"Nothing. I'm fine." Ashley shrugged, as I tried desperately not to blurt out the word *PENIS* at the top of my lungs. And then my eyes fell on our pregnant gym teacher, Coach Cassidy. *Oh my God, did she do that too?* The thought obliterated my resolve. "Ashley! I have to tell you something!"

Now, I don't remember exactly how I phrased it, but whatever I said prompted Ashley to ask, "Wait, what?! There's a hole down there?" So, (1) However I described it couldn't have been great. (2) Ashley's parents failed to educate their daughter about even the most basic biological realities. It's a miracle she made it out of diapers.

Moments like this make me especially grateful for the full-disclosure policy my mother has on sex. And that's even acknowledging the Cheesecake Factory family dinner when she very publicly ranted about an encounter she had with a "penis so crooked it was like his schlong needed braces."

By that evening at dinner, I allowed myself to sink into a cautiously optimistic confidence. Maybe I wouldn't get in trouble for telling! I had been fairly obedient, after all. It's not like I shouted *SPEEEEEEEERM* over the school's PA system. I only told one friend *and* made her pinkie-swear, cross her heart, and hope to die that she wouldn't tell anyone else. As fate would have it, Ashley Adams did not take the hallowed pinkie promise quite as seriously as I hoped. She told her mother. After a quick phone call in the kitchen, my mom marched back to the dinner table, bristling with rage.

"Crystal Adams just called, and she is furious!"

"Crystal Adams . . ." My dad narrowed his eyes trying to place her, and I kept my gaze fixed on my plate. I was in trouble. "Is she the one with the giant fish lips?"

"Yes, but that's not the point." She whipped toward me. "How could you tell Ashley about sex? Kate, you're grounded! After school? No TV. Weekends? You're home studying for a month."

"I'm sorry. I just wanted to talk to someone about it, and Ashley's my friend! Don't be mad at me!" I looked down at the floor and tried to swallow the lump in my throat.

"We're not mad, we're just disappointed." And there they were! The worst words a child can hear—my mother played the disappointment card. In my family, this was reserved for only the most heinous crimes.

The next day at school, Ashley avoided me all morning. I finally asked her at lunch why she was ignoring me. "My mom said you lied to me, and it's true that the stork brings babies to mommies and daddies. She says you made up that story, and that you're a bad girl, and we're not allowed to be friends anymore."

I wanted to cry. Although even as an eight-year-old, part of me was like, *really*? As an adult, I've always wondered: What was her mom's plan? When would the lying end? After high school biology class? College?

Never? If so, Ashley was in for a very surprising wedding night.

It wasn't until college that I even realized my mom's openness with me wasn't standard practice for all mothers and daughters. I was once joking around with my friend Ellen in our dorm about an uncircumcised penis she'd been caught off guard by the night before, and I laughed, "Oh my God, I have to text my mom about this!" Ellen froze. "Are you serious?! You tell your *mom* stuff like that?" *Wait, what? Your mom doesn't know comprehensive details about the genitalia of every guy you've ever dated? Right. Mine doesn't either.*

But back in elementary school, I asked another friend for a pencil in history class, and she gave me the same response: "My mom says I'm not supposed to talk to you anymore." I was stunned; did Ashley tell *everyone*? I choked back tears for the rest of the day, but the bottled-up sobbing broke free in a monsoon of snot and soul-rattling convulsions as soon as I got into the car with my mom.

Ashley's mother had taken it upon herself to start a weird PTA mom crusade against me—the kind of campaign only a woman with far too much time on her perfectly manicured hands could undertake. She was calling every mother in my elementary school class and telling them not to let their kids play with me, that I ruined Ashley's life and was a creepy little girl, obsessed with "carnal pursuits." The fact that the woman wasn't even comfortable calling it "sex" in conversation with adults hints at a whole host of sexually repressed issues, but mostly just makes me feel sorry for her daughter.

Her campaign to brand me with a scarlet N for child Nymphomaniac did not sit well with my mother. She switched into full combat mode. The next morning in the car, she blasted Public Enemy and N.W.A. all the way to school and marched into the headmaster's office for battle instead of heading to work. *Fuck tha police!*

Mr. Thompson calmly listened to a rant that involved a lot of talk about puritanical moms and premarital penises, but he took it well and started chuckling.

"I'm sorry to laugh, but these mothers! Don't worry. I'll talk to Ashley's mom. How do they not understand that sex is all kids talk about at this age!?"

"Exactly! If they lived on a farm, they would have already seen it all live!" Presumably a statement based on my mother's vast childhood experience with farm animal copulation growing up in *Atlantic City, New Jersey.*

Mr. Thompson called Ashley's mom and told her to stop the gossip. And in spite of her mother's "life ruining" concerns, Ashley and I both grew up to be normal teenagers. Not friends, really, just two well-adjusted humans from moms with very different parenting styles. Though I do hope Ashley's mother eventually told her how babies are made or, at the very least, where her vagina is located.

4:05 pm

< Messages **Mother** Details

@CrazyJewishMom

Will pick u up 9pm at bus station. Just sent u another article on alcohol/breast cancer link. No more wine. U and ur boyfriend can smoke pot this weekend. I'll even buy the weed, just stop with the Malbec.

What are you, a drug dealer now?

I'm not like a regular mom, I'm a cool mom.

# My First Fake ID

Most kids get their first fake ID from a sketchy friend with a connection at the DMV. My first fake ID was handed to me directly by my mom when I was twelve years old. Mind you, it wasn't so I could start guzzling 40s and chain-smoking Camel Lights. It was all part of her master plan to help me get into an Ivy League college.

When she is passionate about something, my mother is terrifyingly convincing. Under the right circumstances, she could persuade a vegan to dive headfirst into a platter of ribs. And when I was in sixth grade, she had both me and my father convinced that:

1. Getting into an Ivy League college was the most important thing in the world.

2. We needed to immediately start building my college résumé with extracurricular activities and honors classes.

How could anything you did as a twelve-year-old impact college admissions, you ask? It probably can't, but this is my mom's brain, the same place where a study about trace amounts of carcinogenic material in tap water translated to fifteen years of drinking exclusively bottled water. There was a near divorce whenever my father poured me a glass from the sink.

After a few calls to the top universities (using fake names, so as not to hurt my chances when I would apply *six years later*), my mom identified three extracurriculars that were "hot commodities" for college admissions: tuba, water polo, and crew. Trying to appeal to my artistic nature, she suggested tuba first. What could be cooler than wrapping my body in a giant brass instrument and sentencing myself to ten years of sweating in parades and getting stuck in doorways?

I agreed to try crew, so my mom found a summer

rowing camp at Stanford University for me to attend, but you needed to be fourteen years old in order to enroll. Again, I was twelve, but she signed me up anyway. Screw the rules! This camp was run by actual Stanford coaches! Who knew? Maybe I would even get scouted and recruited for admission! As a lying twelve-year-old.

One morning in the late spring, she woke up the family and herded us into the car for what she described as a "surprise road trip." The last time she said this, we ended up stranded with a flat tire in Compton. Why? My mother wanted to try her luck at a liquor store that was famous for selling winning lottery tickets.

When she took the Maple Avenue exit from the I-10 freeway, I was relieved and excited. I instantly knew we were on our way to the Santee Alley, a literal alley in the middle of downtown Los Angeles. It is a bustling three-block thoroughfare lined with stores and pop-up stands, hawking everything from bootlegged DVDs to replica handbags to live animals.

"Oh my God, YESSS! Please, please, please, please, please, PLEASE, Mom, can we get a turtle today?!!"

"We'll see. But first we're going to get you a fake ID!"

"What?!" My father turned to her in the passenger seat.

"Relax, Michael. Don't go get a shotgun yet! Your daughter's not going out clubbing. It's for the rowing camp she's going to this summer. They said we need to bring proof of age."

My mother parked the car in a garage a few blocks away from the alley's main entrance, and we fought our way through the crowded streets. I'd like to point out here that my mother is a terrible criminal. The alley was a place people went to eat street meat (that usually resulted in diarrhea) and buy knockoff handbags, not a place where terrorists went to buy forged government documents. And what was her master plan? To walk up to random people on the street and ask them if they could sell her a counterfeit birth certificate? That was precisely her plan.

My mother went from vendor to vendor, slowly examining the merchandise at each table until a salesman approached her and tried to sell her the fake Chanel or Prada bag in her hands.

"You like that? That's best-quality leather. Top quality." My mother—again, the world's least-smooth criminal—made this transition: "Actually, I'm looking for something a little *hotter*?" Each time she said this, the salesman in question gave her a quizzical look. One of them asked, "What you mean? Like, sexy dresses? I do bags, no dresses." My mother's criminal shorthand, ripped from movies like *Rush Hour 2* and *Blue Streak*, was not translating to the real world. We were halfway through the seventh iteration of my mom's illicit routine when it landed.

". . . Actually, I'm looking for something a little *hotter*?"

"Okay, mamma, what you need?" A towering West African man nodded at her knowingly.

"I need a fake ID."

The guy looked her up and down. "You a cop? What you need a fake ID for? You look forty!" My mother pulled the man into a hug.

"Forty! Honey, thank you! Michael, did you hear that? This guy thinks I look forty!" My dad rolled his eyes, and my mom pointed at me. "It's not for me, it's for my daughter."

"All right, cool mamma!" The guy grinned. "Okay, okay. Follow me."

He led us through throngs of people in the crowded alley to a desolate, boarded-up warehouse fifteen blocks away. I grabbed my mother's arm.

"Mom, this feels sketchy. Maybe we should go back."

"Oh my God, what do you think is gonna happen? You're gonna get murdered?" *I mean, maybe. Yeah.* "You need to stop watching *Law & Order: SVU.* Mamma's here. I'll kill anyone who looks at you the wrong way."

My dad, who was no longer surprised by any of my mother's schemes, just shrugged and told me not to worry. The salesman banged three times on the entrance to the warehouse and shouted something in a language I couldn't understand. After a few moments, the door swung open and an old wrinkled woman was glaring at us from her perch on a rickety stool. She took us in and nodded, opening the door just wide enough for us to pass.

We followed the man into an enormous warehouse, an open space at least five stories high. Every surface was covered in counterfeit designer handbags. It looked like a Technicolor shrine to the Almighty Purse. My mother stopped short, having arrived in her version of heaven, and my dad groaned.

"Oh my God! Look at these bags!" She was pursegasming.

After some intense haggling, my mother followed the salesman into an office in the back of the warehouse, clutching two replica Chanel bags. She motioned for us to hurry. As we entered, an Asian man with a bright blond mohawk looked up at us from his desk. My mother smiled.

"Hi, we need identification for my daughter here."

The man looked over at my gawky twelve-year-old frame and my oily face with an angry whitehead begging to be popped on my chin.

"Nobody's gonna believe that girl's twenty-one!"

"No, no . . . we need a birth certificate or a passport or something. It should say she's fourteen."

"Uh, we don't do that shit here. We make fakes for like clubs and shit." The guy looked at her like she was smoking the crystal meth that they also didn't sell. Because again, these people were replica-handbag salesmen, *not* terrorist document forgers on an NSA watch list. My mother paused.

"You know what? Just give her a driver's license. We'll make her look sixteen."

"Okay, I'll take your money!" He laughed and rose from the desk, grabbing his camera. He motioned for me to stand up against the smudged white backdrop. "Okay, smile!" I did, revealing a metallic smorgasbord, and the man physically recoiled. "Okay, don't smile."

When we showed up at Stanford for crew camp a few weeks later, my braces were off, my mother had painted my face in dramatic makeup, and she dressed me in platform shoes. At the registration desk she offered, "Kate just turned sixteen! Always looked young for her age. She hates it now, but let me tell you, she'll be happy about it when she's pushing forty!"

The college student manning the check-in table never even asked us to provide ID and just trusted that I was a very tiny sixteen-year-old girl with no breasts and poor makeup-application skills. She handed me my registration packet and said with a smile, "Welcome to Stanford."

STANFORD
ROWING CAMP
SESSION 2
2001

2:06 pm

< Messages **Mother** Details

@CrazyJewishMom

HOLY CRAMPS I'M DYING

It's like a full on battle scene happening here. STAR WARS: RETURN OF THE UTERUS.

THE OVARIES STRIKE BACK

# I Am Woman

My mother takes special occasions as seriously as Paula Deen takes butter. Every Thanksgiving, she hosts a fleet of forty relatives at our house, serving dinner on her favorite (NOT dishwasher-safe) cranberry Spode china. My mom barely allows people to eat off these dishes, so after dinner she chases helpful guests out of the kitchen and hand-washes over two hundred individual pieces of china. Usually until 4 a.m.

Birthdays are no different. When I turned three, she hired a children's party entertainer to come to our beach bash as Ariel from *The Little Mermaid*. She convinced this poor actress to dunk herself in the ocean (in January) before walking up to the party from the sand. You know, to make it authentic for the three-year-olds. For Hanukkah, she lights all ten of our menorahs and invites her guests to bring their own. By the eighth night every year, we have burned through a minimum of five hundred candles and have set off at least one fire alarm. It's a miracle we haven't burned down the house.

And these are just regular old holidays that happen every year! Can you imagine how she might handle a once-in-a-lifetime celebration like, I don't know, a wedding? I can! Because she has already floated the following ideas about my hypothetical nuptials:

1. "Why not wear a black dress? Make your bridesmaids wear white! Let them look like heifers, and you look thin!"
2. "We're not doing that solemn 'here comes the bride' crap, marching you down the aisle like you're property. We're going to have a choreographed dance to something upbeat like 'I like big butts and I cannot lie!!! You other brothers can't deny!'"
3. "Oh! You'll get married at Lucy the Elephant!!! You can say your vows on the top!" Lucy the Elephant is a decaying historical landmark on the beach in Margate, New Jersey, just out-

side of Atlantic City. It is a six-story novelty building shaped like an elephant:

Yeah. I'm pretty terrified about getting married.

Thankfully, she hasn't had too many once-in-a-lifetime celebrations to plan thus far, though there have been a few. And this brings me to my mother's handling of my first menstrual cycle.

In fifth grade, my best friend, Molly, told me she had gotten her period, and I was incredibly jealous. Sixth grade passed with Aunt Flo visiting every single girl in my class but me, and I was riddled with tampon envy.

As seventh grade started to zoom by, and my underwear remained spotless, I got angry. *Come on, uterus, get your shit together!* I wanted so badly to reach that milestone, to join in on the fun, complaining with the rest of the girls about feminine products and cramps. And who knew? Maybe my boobs would come in too.

I was almost fourteen when I dropped my pants in the bathroom and found a little red stain in my underwear. In all of my hot-pink fantasies about girl talk and Midol, I had glossed over the blood and hadn't even considered that I might be alone, in a public restroom, when I got my period for the first time. I was frightened and embarrassed.

The bathroom was at Renaissance Kids, where I was getting extra algebra help after school. I shoved some toilet paper between my legs and waddled back over to the classroom, where the instructor, Anna, was scribbling an equation on the whiteboard. I cracked open the door. "Excuse me, Anna? Can I talk to you for a second? Um, in private?" My cheeks must have been quite pink, because she looked concerned as she walked with me to the back of the office. I mumbled that I had gotten my period and asked her to call my mom, while my classmates undoubtedly strained to hear what exciting drama was afoot.

They didn't have to strain terribly hard though, because my mother was still in the parking lot and came running back into the office when Anna called. She swung open the door and bounded toward me with her arms open wide. "Ah! She's a woman!" I was expecting a hug, but she slapped me across the face (more of a tap), and shouted, "MAZEL TOV!"

For those of you who are not Jewish, my mother was not having a psychotic break or rehearsing for a role in a dramatic telenovela. She was practicing a Jewish tradition called "The Menstrual Slap." It's not exactly clear where this tradition comes from or why it's done, but I've heard explanations that range from it being "a woman's warning to guard her gates against premarital entry" to a reminder that "a woman's life is filled with pain." Exactly what a hormonal teenage girl needs to hear. *You think Jill McCarthy making fun of your zits is bad? Well, wait until childbirth.*

"I'm so excited! My little girl is a woman! But don't

think that means it's time to start letting boys stick their tongues down your throat!"

"Shh! Mother!" Some of the kids from my classroom down the hall were giggling. I grabbed my backpack. "Okay, can we go now?"

"Who do you think we are, the Rockefellers? I'm paying seventy-five dollars for this class!" She rustled around in her bag for a moment and thrust a tampon in my face. "Here, shove this up your hooha, and get back in there!"

"Mom, I don't know how!"

"Relax, I'll show you." She shooed me back into the bathroom.

After a few minutes, including a live demonstration, I figured out the tampon and was back in class, trying to concentrate on algebraic functions but stressing about whether or not I was leaking onto my chair. As soon as the hour expired, I rushed out to the car where my mother was waiting.

"So, how do you feel?"

"I don't know. The same." I squirmed. I was actually feeling terrible. I'm not sure if it was the blood (the sight always makes me pass out), the concern about humiliating myself with a period stain at school one day, or the larger realization that I was now capable of growing another human, but I was anxious.*

"You're fine for another hour or so; we'll practice putting another one in when we get to the house. SEAT-BELT!"

"Okay, okay. Hurry. I want to go home."

"Hold your horses! I'm going to stop at CVS and pick up some more tampons. I don't know if I have enough at the house for both of us *big fertile women*!"

We walked to the tampon aisle, and I grabbed a box of the Tampax Pearls that I had seen in all my friends' bathrooms. My mother swatted at my hand. "Not so fast, Miss Kate!" She glanced around and flagged a middle-aged pharmacy employee wearing a CVS white coat. "Oh, excuse me, sir?"

"Can I help you?" The man paused, and walked over to us.

"Yes, thank you! My daughter just got her period,

* The "growing-another-human" thing would be moot for many years to come, in light of my Supervirgin status throughout high school.

and I'm wondering if there is a specific brand of tampons that's better suited for young girls? Maybe something organic?" She smiled at him, and I cringed.

"Standard tampons should be just fine. You could start out with slim ones, but there's no reason to unless she experiences discomfort with the regular size."

"You tell us, Kate, did the one you put in earlier hurt?" My mouth fell open, and I headed back out to the car without responding. As I sped down the feminine products aisle, my mom turned back to the man. "I guess that's a no!"

I waited, fuming in the car, but as milestones with my mother go, it could have been far worse. In fact, it had been worse. During the summer before seventh grade, after months of pleading, she finally agreed to buy me my first bra (that I in no way needed). I imagined we'd go somewhere fun and sexy like Victoria's Secret. Instead, she took me to a little hole-in-the-wall bra shop at a suburban strip mall. The centerpiece of the store was an aging, borderline-obese man. His voice was hoarse from years of cigarettes, and he would shout out his (always accurate) estimation of your bra size when you walked in the door. As I entered, he barked, "Get those mosquito bites outta here!" I didn't have long to feel embarrassed though, because a transgender woman came in right after me, and the man screamed, "Thirty-eight double D! Chanel, you finally got the titties put in! It's about time . . . one more Wonderbra, and I woulda shoved those implants in myself!"

So this was better.

By the time we arrived home, the sun had set. I noticed that my dad's car was missing from the driveway, and the lights were off in our house.

"Where's Dad?"

"The market? Who knows! Shoot, I've gotta pee!" She closed the car door and rushed ahead toward the house. "Come to my bathroom. We can change your tampon after I pee!" I glanced around the neighborhood, thankful that no one was out walking a dog or getting their mail.

As the front door swung open, the lights flipped on, and Shania Twain's voice was singing, "Man! I feel like a woman!" My mother was dancing in front of the door, wearing a bright red party hat and swinging tampons by their strings. My dad was standing between a bouquet of crimson balloons and the dining room table, smiling uncomfortably. I looked around, and the entire house was decorated for a "period party." There were tampons taped to walls, boxes of panty liners, and Midol in a cute little basket on the coffee table. Red dots of glitter were sprinkled over every surface, and cherry-colored streamers were hung all over the room.

My mother danced over to me, strapped a party hat on my head, and hung a silky red sash across my body.

"Oh my GOD! Mom, you told Dad!?" I shouted over the music.

"Oh relax, it's just your father!" She shrugged, uninterested in my humiliation.

"How did you even do this?"

"I've had these decorations since you were in the third grade. Took you long enough!" She blew a glittering party horn in my face. Apparently, my mother had been planning my period party for years, with different contingency plans for different "period getting" scenarios. We walked over to my dad, who had thrown together this mortifying little event in her absence.

"So, Michael! Tell her what's for dinner!" He blushed and, after a quick smack on the shoulder, recited the period-themed menu. It included clams in red sauce. She couldn't resist, adding, "And we got *red* velvet cake for dessert! But easy on the cake, honey. Sticks directly on the hips. Welcome to womanhood."

As always, my mother's enthusiasm was as contagious as the flu. By the time we wrapped up the dance party to her "girl power" CD and sat down for dinner, I was fully infected. All my anxiety about tampons and birthing babies was gone; even my father was singing along with us to *Gypsy*'s "Everything's Coming Up Roses" by the end of the night. And this is one of the things I love most about my mother: she knows just how to make me smile, and exactly when I need to the most. That said, while it's wonderful to know my mom will be there for me when I have my inevitable wedding-day anxiety attack, I really hope she doesn't try to sneak "cherry popping" sundaes onto the menu. Let's be real: that ship has sailed.

9:40 pm

< Messages **Mother** Details

@CrazyJewishMom

Awww looking through old pix and found this one from ur play! If only this were real . . .

Mother, I was playing a drunk, single, pregnant sorority girl in that sketch . . .

At least u were pregnant

# "Sing Out, Louise!"

*"If you're going to commit to something, you better do whatever it takes to make it happen."*

—KIM FRIEDMAN,
at least once a month my entire life

This is a mantra my mother both practiced and preached. As a fervent antiwar activist in the late '60s, she was arrested three times while protesting the Vietnam war. One of the demonstrations that my mother dreamed up involved collecting severed, bloody animal parts from a butcher and then leading a pack of angry activists to Broadway, where they flung blood and meat onto theatergoers arriving to see "frivolous" musicals. All while screaming, "BLOOD IN HANOI? BLOOD ON BROADWAY! BLOOD IN HANOI? BLOOD ON BROADWAY!" When her comrades suggested using red paint instead of actual animal blood, my mother responded with "DO OUR SOLDIERS BLEED PAINT?!"

The fact that this "street theater" was *not* one of the three protests she got arrested for (1) makes you wonder what the hell she did to get arrested those other times (I asked, and she was very vague) and (2) illustrates the lengths she will go to once she has decided to commit to something.

*Kate, if you're going to play water polo, why just swim well when you can also file your fingernails into points and scratch your opponents underwater?**

*If you're going to enter a costume contest on Halloween, why dress as a princess when your father can build you a custom lime-green boom box that actually plays the "Macarena"?*

*If you're going to run for student council, why just make a speech when you can also wear a Supergirl costume and sing?* In fairness to her, I won that election.

The "whatever it takes" idea is something that manifested in every aspect of her parenting, but there is

* I failed out of rowing camp, so I had to play water polo for my college admissions résumé. Per my mother.

no better example I can point to than an incident my family refers to as The 8th Grade Play Affair.

When the drama department at my middle school, Harvard-Westlake, announced that the spring play would be *A Midsummer Night's Dream*, my mother had a happy seizure. I was excited too, as I had been fantasizing about playing Hermia since my mother first read the play to me in elementary school. It was my dream part.

Unfortunately, the chance of me getting that role was about as likely as getting abducted and anally probed by aliens. It was widely understood that seventh and eighth graders never got the leads. The main parts were always awarded to the ninth graders, who had paid their dues. My mother's response to this unspoken policy: "Well, if it's *unspoken*, it's not a real policy, now, is it?"

The day after the initial audition, I paced alongside all the other hopefuls during lunch. We were waiting next to the drama department bulletin board to find out who had gotten called back for a second tryout. Now, if you've ever met a theater nerd, you probably know that "theater nerd waiting to find out if they got a part" is not a theater nerd at his or her best. Add to that the fact that some of these kids were actual working actors in Hollywood, and worse, some of them had *parents* who were A-list actors, directors, and writers, and you can start to understand the atmosphere and the pressure. One girl actually threw up, and she wasn't even bulimic! All the faux camaraderie had evaporated, and the vicious little animals that we were emerged.

Two minutes before the lunch period was over, the director sprinted out, pinned up the list, and scurried back into her office, wisely locking the door between herself and a sea of angsty teenagers. A mosh pit instantly formed around the callbacks list, and I couldn't see over the crowd. I was jumping up and down, trying to catch a glimpse over everyone's shoulders, when Larry Glassman turned toward me, braces gleaming.

"Congrats, Kate! We both got callbacks!"

He had auditioned for Lysander, Hermia's love interest in the play. My heart fluttered, and not just because of the news that I had gotten a callback for Hermia. Nerdy, sweet Larry and I had been in the ensemble casts of both shows in seventh grade together, and I was in love with him, metal mouth, crackling pubescent voice, and all. He had a quiet attractiveness that none of the other girls had noticed yet, but oh boy, I had. I blushed.

"Thanks, Larry! Congrats to you too!" He squeezed my shoulder warmly, inciting a minor cardiac event, and left me pining after him. I stepped up to the bulletin board to confirm the results for myself and immediately ran off to call my mom.

Her response? "Start memorizing your lines."

When we walked through our front door after water polo practice that evening, my dad was sitting on the couch in the living room where we always rehearsed. My mother flung her arm out, pointing toward the kitchen.

"Michael, out!"

My dad looked up, remote in hand. "But I'm watching—"

"Get your butt out of here! Go make dinner or something. Healthy."

"Kim, come on, there's only a minute left in th—"

"Oh, I didn't realize *boxing* was more important to you than your only daughter's future. You know what? Never mind, I totally understand. You just finish your show, and if Kate doesn't get the part? She doesn't get the part! It's not like getting the lead in this play could make the difference between her being able to get into an Ivy League college, having a fabulous career, meeting an intelligent man to breed with . . . and becoming a high school dropout! You just finish your show, Michael, by all means, we'll wait."

My father, in an effort to avoid getting roped into another one of our marathon rehearsals, shut off the television and wandered into the kitchen. In his mind, even washing dishes would be better than seven hours of playing his daughter's love interest.

"Okay, Kate! I have an amazing idea!" Amazing? Her last "amazing" idea involved trying to vacation on the cheap and getting us stuck in a foreign country in a house filled with flying cockroaches. So you can understand my skepticism.

The scene the drama teacher selected for the callback was between Hermia and Lysander; it also happened to be the pinnacle of sexual tension between the two characters. My mom rustled through the pages in her hand and pointed to one highlighted section of the script.

"Here, this line."

"Which one?" I walked over and saw that she was talking about the climax of the scene, in which Hermia is trying to resist the urge to sleep with Lysander.

"I just know all the girls are going to wimp out on this part and not really do it full out."

"Okay, so what's your idea?"

"Well . . . instead of just hugging him or something stupid like that, I think you should get a running start, jump on him, wrap your legs around his waist, and actually kiss him full out. Stick your tongue in his mouth if you can."

And there it was, the old "whatever it takes" rearing its (in this case, sexually aggressive) head. *If you're going to audition for a play, why just act well when you can also perform an over-the-top sexy stunt to make sure you get the part?* The most frustrating aspect of my mother's "whatever it takes" moments is that they almost always work. And in this case, the end was something I desperately wanted, independent of my mother.

That said, I was thirteen, so I also desperately wanted to avoid making an idiot of myself in front of a large group of mean teenagers.

"Are you insane? In front of everyone? Absolutely not! No way!" I folded my arms.

"Kate, I realize it's a little over the top, but it's the only shot you have at getting this part. Yeah, you're good, probably better than everyone else auditioning, but you've gotta do something big if you're going to beat out Carly for the lead."

Of course she was annoyingly right. Carly was one of the other girls who had gotten a callback for Hermia, and she was my main competition for the role. She was a very talented young actress and also a ninth grader, so if she didn't completely blow the audition, she had a 90 percent chance of getting cast. "Come on, let's at least rehearse it this way, and you can decide tomorrow. Let's just try it."

We spent the next three hours running the scene, before I collapsed onto my bed in a heap of anxious exhaustion. After school the next day, I shuffled into the black box theater where the auditions were being held, with everyone else who had gotten a callback for the play. My mother was a professional television director, so I trusted her instincts, but would I have the nerve to actually do it?

All day I had been obsessing over who my scene partner would be. I was facing a Russian roulette of hormone-crazed pubescent theater-nerd lips. I silently scanned the room and found everyone who had been called back for Lysander: Tom Michaelson, Bobby Friedburg, and, of course, dreamboat Larry Glassman.

Tom would be the ideal candidate. He was gay, he was my friend, and he was still publicly pretending to be into girls, so it was a win-win. Bobby was in ninth grade and over six feet tall, so at (optimistically) five foot three, I felt like that was a setup for logistical failure. And, *OH GOD*, what if it were Larry? Would I have the nerve to stick my tongue in his mouth? I had already lost my smooching virginity way back in seventh grade during a game of Truth or Dare at a bat mitzvah (no tongue though). But, yeah, I knew a thing or two about locking lips. Larry, on the other hand, was a late bloomer, and everyone knew he hadn't kissed anyone yet.

Someone tapped me on the shoulder, and I turned to find Larry giving me a nervous thumbs-up. "Come on, sit with me over here!" He smiled at me excitedly. "You ready?!"

I fought the nausea welling up in my throat and sat down next to him on the floor. The auditions began, and after about forty-five minutes of acting that ranged from Corky St. Clair–level terrible to Maggie Smith–level fantastic, it was time for the Hermia and Lysander scene.

Ms. Benson, the director, climbed back up onto the stage with the clipboard. "Okay, settle down, everyone! Shhh! Okay, up first, for Hermia and Lysander . . . Carly, you're reading Hermia; Bobby, you're reading Lysander."

I sat back and watched Carly absolutely nail her audition—she hit every beat of the scene perfectly and had all seventy competitive teenagers in the room giggling. My mother's parting words from that morning at car pool rang in my ears: "Come on!! Just go for it! If you do it like we rehearsed, you're going to get the part."

I watched as Ms. Benson stepped back on stage, wiping tears of laughter from her eyes, and I knew I would have to go through with it.

"Wow, great work, guys!" Ms. Benson smiled.

I willed her to call Tom and me up to perform, and it occurred to me that if this worked, I might have a future in mind control. I wasn't sure I could actually go through with the stunt if I had to do the scene with Larry. She glanced down at the clipboard, and I held my breath.

"All right, let's see. Tom, get up here. You're reading Lysander. And Hermia . . . Sara Jane, you're up!"

Smiling, Larry nudged me and leaned in, whispering, "Awesome! I was hoping we'd get paired up!"

*STOP BEING NICE TO ME, LARRY! GODDAMN*

*IT, CAN'T YOU SEE I'M TRYING TO CONVINCE MYSELF TO JUMP YOUR BONES!?*

Soon it was our turn. From the moment we started the scene, our chemistry was palpable. I remember thinking, *Wow, I might actually be getting more laughs than Carly.* I hesitated at the big line, wondering if I even needed the stunt to get the part. My mother's voice flashed into my head again: "Come on, Kate! Don't back down now! Whatever it takes!" *Screw it.*

Larry's eyes widened as I raced toward him, but he absorbed the shock of my weight wrapped around his waist and the firm press of my mouth against his with surprising ease. The audience leapt to its feet and started shrieking—50 percent shock, 50 percent laughter. And Larry's mouth was everything I had dreamed it would be.

So did the end justify the means? It feels odd to answer *yes* when the means involved stealing the mouth virginity of an eighth grader, and the end was a leading role in a middle school production of *A Midsummer Night's Dream*. But I got the part, so technically, yeah, another one of my mother's "whatever it takes" moments was a success.

That said, Carly got the guy. She and Larry went on to be the first-ever younger man–older woman scandal in our drama club, so I guess it was a mixed bag.

4:35 pm

< Messages **Mother** Details

@CrazyJewishMom

Omg spawn, where did u find that pix w/ me & the gator? Send me so I can put on my FB!

I loved her! So happy she was rescued!

I wanted to keep her but she's happier in Miami!

# The Pound Diaries

Biologically speaking, I am my mother's only child. In my mother's eyes, however, I have loads of siblings! Of course, that's only if you count our pack of five dogs and two cats as humans, which my mom definitely does. Her intense love and scrutiny extend to each and every member of our family, no matter how much some of us may drool.

Just look at her boundless devotion to our (arguably psychotic) Chihuahua named Thor. When he started

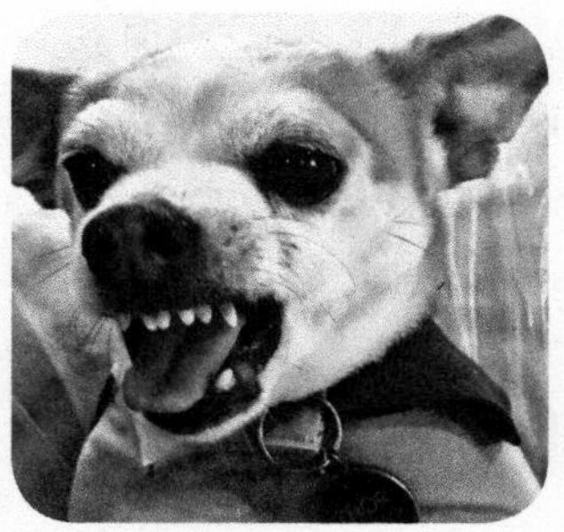

viciously growling at walls and seeing things that weren't there, thousands were spent on doggy therapy bills, doggy Prozac, and doggy acupuncture. (Which is a real thing!) Once someone is part of the Friedman-Siegel family, they will never be left behind. Canine, feline, or otherwise.

Practically speaking, what this means is that each time our front door opens, a gaggle of violently yelping Chihuahuas alternate between piddling, wagging their tails, and humping legs with the kind of excitement I'd imagine Snow White felt when Prince Charming woke her up (though I doubt Walt Disney allowed any humping). My mother always shouts a greeting over the pandemonium and shrugs her shoulders as if to say, "What can you do, *right*?"

In fact, there is a lot she could do. For instance, the first time my boyfriend visited, she could have left the dogs in my father's office, instead of allowing my siblings to gangbang his ankles.

On the bright side, though, we never have to worry about Jehovah's Witnesses.

And the cats? Humans and dogs alike understand that the feline occupants of my parents' home have first right of refusal for all horizontal surfaces. But no one has ever ruled the house quite like the all-white cat we inventively named Snowflake. Every parent has a favorite child, whether they're willing to admit it or not, and when I was growing up, my mom's heart unquestionably belonged to this little furball.

Snowflake was just a three-week-old kitten when we found her cowering in the middle of a twisty street in the Hollywood Hills. My mother swerved to the side of the road and leapt out of her car, scooping Snowflake into her arms.

That tiny kitten looked up with one green eye and one crusted blue eye, her malnourished frame covered in fleas, and my mom fell in love. She spent the next month nursing her back to health, bottle-feeding her, and composing songs for her. Hell, she practically breast-fed her.

And when Snowflake grew up, my mother treated this cat better than she treated me—she bought cat toys like it was her job, she brought Snowflake to "take your child to work day" instead of me, she forced my dad to prepare her home-cooked meals (mostly wild-caught salmon), and she even bought her a special orthopedic cat bed.

So, when Snowflake died suddenly, my mother was devastated. Like, borderline psychotic break devastated. Unfortunately, her grief didn't manifest with tears or weight gain; her anguish presented itself in the middle of the cat funeral being held in our backyard when she leapt into the tiny cat grave my father was filling and snatched the box containing Snowflake's ashes from the dirt.

"No!" My mother clutched the container to her chest. "She can't be in the cold ground like this!"

From then on, whenever one of our animals passed away, a place on our mantel was cleared for a new designer urn. At this point, our fireplace is 90 percent animal remains. I just thank God my mother never got hooked on taxidermy.

Like most normal humans who lose a family pet,

my dad thought it would be a good idea to get a replacement cat (after the appropriate grieving period). When he suggested this at dinner one night, making sure to qualify the idea with, "Not that anyone could ever replace Snowflake . . ." my mother spat at him, "So if you die, I should just go out the next day, find another husband, and pretend you never existed?" *Grief takes many forms.*

That weekend, my father and I dragged my mom to the city animal shelter, and a woman named Pat with a military haircut greeted us at the door of the cat room with a brusque: "Do not open the cages. If you want to see a cat, talk to me."

It was a bright, fluorescently lit space that only marginally made you feel like you were gagging on the scent of cat urine. The walls of the small room were lined with cages, and my mother was the last to enter. Her arms were folded tightly across her chest, her sour attitude palpable.

I noticed a cage in the far corner of the room. It was barely visible, and intentionally pushed off to the side.

Inside was a tiny all-white kitten with blue eyes, even smaller than Snowflake was when we found her on the street.

"Oh my God! Mom, come look at this kitten!"

"We don't need another animal—" She trailed off abruptly as she came face-to-face with Snowflake's spitting image. "Oh my God!" She reached toward the lever on the cage.

"I said, don't open the cages!" Pat shouted from behind us.

"Oh, right. Can we see this one?" My mom gestured toward the kitten.

"No."

"Why not? Is she already adopted?"

My mother turned back to the cage, clearly convinced that this kitten was her precious Snowflake reincarnated.

"No, we have to put it down. It's sick, and it's too young to survive on its own."

"So you're just going to *kill* her? What's wrong with her?"

I could see my mother's blood pressure rising as Pat stepped between her and Snowflake Reincarnated.

In Pat's defense, the sad truth is that many animals, even perfectly *healthy* ones, are euthanized at animal shelters across the country every year due to overcrowding.

"It's just too weak, and we think it's got intestinal parasites . . . listen, just go find another cat. This one's too sick to adopt." Pat shoved the cage farther out of view.

"You people call this an animal shelter?" my mother asked, her voice getting louder with each word. "Ha! More like an execution chamber! I'm not leaving until you let me adopt that kitten!" Her skin turned three shades redder than I had ever seen it get.

"Can't do it."

Now, I'm not sure if this is an official government policy or if Pat was just an asshole who didn't want to do extra paperwork, but she shrugged and clearly was not going to budge.

"Oh, really? Well, then, how about I call all the local

news stations, and you can explain to them what part of your job tells you to murder innocent kittens when there are families who are begging you to let them adopt them!"

"Okay, Mom, let's just take it easy for a second." I touched her arm.

"Take it easy? I will handcuff myself to these cages before I let them murder that kitten."

As someone who had been arrested on multiple occasions for sit-ins and protests for causes she felt strongly about, my mother was not bluffing.

"Okay, let's just all calm down here," my dad intervened, recognizing that my mom's rage-o-meter was dialed up to ASSAULT.

"I'm perfectly calm." Pat folded her arms.

My mother paused briefly and then began to violently sob. This should have been the first red flag, as I had never once seen her cry. She was shrieking with apparent grief and turned toward Pat, sniffling.

"I'm so s-sorry about that," she said. "I just lost my baby cat, Snowflake, and I'm just—devastated . . . I'm so s-sorry—"

And there was red flag number two! To my knowledge, my mother has apologized a grand total of five times in her life. And one of those times involved a member of the National Guard and tear gas.

"Can you please forgive me?! OH GOD, MY SNOWFLAKE!!!!!!!"

Her words dissolved into more over-the-top bawling, and she threw herself across Pat's chest, pulling the woman into a bear hug.

"Uh, that's okay." Pat awkwardly patted my mother's arm as she tried to inch away. "Hey, I'll let you guys take a look around. Just come get me when you want to see a cat." The door swung shut behind her.

My father and I walked over to my wailing mother, preparing to console her. As soon as the latch on the door clicked shut, she lifted her head and shrugged us off.

"Is she gone? Give me your purse."

"What? Are you okay?"

She yanked the messenger bag from my shoulder.

"What are you doing, Mom?!"

"Michael, go stand over there. Look out the door

and tell me if she's coming back. Kate, you too!" She glanced over her shoulder at the door and hurried to Snowflake Reincarnated's cage. *My mother was about to steal a cat from the pound.*

"Mom, STOP!" I reached for my purse. "No, you absolutely cannot do this!"

"Just guard the door."

"Kim! Move away from the cat cages."

"Michael, don't even start with me. They're going to MURDER Snowflake!"

Before either of us could intervene, my mom opened the latch, lifted the trembling kitten out of the cage, and gently placed it in the bottom of my messenger bag.

Unfortunately, when my mother closed the flap over Snowflake Reincarnated, we discovered that Snowflake Reincarnated did not like being carried in a small, dark handbag with peppermint gum fumes and spare change. In fact, Snowflake Reincarnated hated that.

We also discovered that the sickly, tiny body of Snowflake Reincarnated housed lungs on par with

Pavarotti. As soon as the bag was closed, the kitten began meowing at an eardrum-shredding volume.

My mother, my father, and I all froze, impressed as much as we were panicked. For those unfamiliar with the sound of a cat in distress, it most closely resembles the sounds a woman makes during natural childbirth.

We tore out of the cat room, while Snowflake Reincarnated wailed. The only way out of the shelter was through the dog run—a narrow hallway surrounded on both sides by long rows of dog kennels.

Now, as you may have heard, cats and dogs sometimes don't get along. I have never been more keenly aware of this concept than when my mother grabbed my wrist and pulled me into an all-out sprint down this hallway. My dad followed, and as we ran, Snowflake Reincarnated meowed like no one was watching, and fifty-plus dogs erupted into a symphony of woofing. The deep barks of pit bulls tangled with the sharp yips of terriers to create a truly earsplitting uproar as we charged down the hall.

I glanced over my shoulder as we reached the door.

Pat emerged at the far end of the corridor and ran over to the first cage, trying to figure out what had caused all the dogs to riot.

We rushed outside before she spotted us and made it out to the car unscathed. My mom carefully reached down into the messenger bag and pulled Snowflake Reincarnated onto her lap, clutching the kitten protectively against her chest.

"Drive, Michael!"

"Kim! Have you lost your mind!?" He sat in the driver's seat, dumbfounded.

"She's an innocent kitten!" My mom looked back at the shelter door.

"Enough!" I said. "We don't have time to argue right now! Dad . . . it's done, we need to get out of here. Mom . . . you're a lunatic, we're never taking you outside again. Now let's go!!!"

My father peeled out of the parking lot and floored it all the way to our veterinarian. We also stopped to pick up medication, kitten formula, and every accessory Petco had to offer, and I'm happy to report that we did in fact nurse Snowflake Reincarnated back to health. The kitten went on to live a long, happy life as a *male* cat named Buster. (Because we busted him out of the pound! *GET IT?*) Buster was sick for a long time and needed a great deal of attention once we got him home, but he was family the second my mom looked into his hopeful little eyes.

And this is one of the best things my mother has ever taught me: you never, ever give up on a family member. Even if it turns out that *she* has a cat penis and is not the reincarnated spirit of your beloved dead pet after all.

8:01 am

< Messages **Mother** Details

@CrazyJewishMom

I literally just got into a wrestling match in the middle of the supermarket

????? I'm going to need you to provide more detail

A lady tried to kidnap MY turkey.

So you FOUGHT her??

Don't worry. I won.

# Stalking 101

When I was growing up, I relied on my mother to lull me to sleep every night with a new installment from her original bedtime saga, *The Teeny Tiny Tim Chronicles.* Each chapter would begin the same way: "Once upon a time, there was a teeeeeeeeny teeny teeny tiny teeny tiny teeny tiny little mouse, and his name was Teeny Tiny Tim . . ." and would end with, "and when he grew up, he went to Harvard, Yale, or Princeton, and had a wonderful career and a happy life!"

The stories centered on a mouse called Teeny Tiny Tim and his mother, Ethel the (human) Opera Singer, who lived on the Upper West Side of Manhattan in a beautiful apartment with a terrace that overlooked Central Park. The Teeny Tiny Tim character was living my mother's idealized version of my life in that moment—if I was playing water polo, Tiny Tim was the captain of his tiny mouse team. If I was studying for a history test in school, Tiny Tim was on the National Mall, meeting with the president.

Recently, I was thinking about these stories and realized that there was an interesting thematic trend: stalking. This was a crucial part of the narrative for about 95 percent of them. For instance, after being told by a Broadway director that a mouse would never be cast in one of his shows, Ethel and Tim chased him all around Manhattan, shouting, “YOU’RE A MICE-IST! LET ALL SPECIES ACT!! SPECIES BLIND CASTING!!!” Of course, Tim got the part. In another story, he wasn’t allowed to ice-skate at the Central Park rink. Ethel and Tim marched into the mayor’s office and refused to leave until he reversed the city’s controversial “mice on ice” ban. In another rather prescient installment, Tim and Ethel waited outside of the prestigious Dalton School after Tim was denied admission. As soon as the headmaster emerged, Tim made an impassioned case for Mice-ffirmative Action. The next day Tiny Tim was dressed in his tiny Dalton uniform, holding his tiny mouse pencil, crushing Advanced Placement calculus like any other mammal in the room.

And this early emphasis (brainwashing) makes sense, in light of how much stalking we ultimately did, especially as it related to my education and, more specifically, to my campaign to get into college.

During high school, my mother and I embarked on an utterly miserable week of college tours that nearly led to a matricidal incident on I-95 South. Anyone who has gone on a college tour with their mother can probably relate to the rage-inducing claustrophobia that comes from spending a week in a car with the one person in the world more invested in college admissions than you. Between the teen angst and the menopausal mood swings, the car becomes a pressure cooker of hormones, ready to explode at the slightest perceived criticism. That said, I'm willing to bet that *your* mother did not map out the local Fantastic Sams in each college town and force you to get a blowout before every interview.

All the screaming and murderous fantasies became

worthwhile the moment I walked onto Princeton's campus. Maybe it was the university's undergraduate focus, maybe it was the preppy man candy, or perhaps it was the vast selection of snacks at the twenty-four-hour Wawa on campus (The Wa!), but Princeton became my first choice. The crusade to get in overshadowed everything else in my life.

I attended every information session Princeton offered in the state of California and met with any Princeton alumnus in the Los Angeles metropolitan area who would agree to see me. Literally anyone. I even spent an hour with a shy urologist, who was as perplexed as I was to be talking about his pre-med experiences with a student who was about as interested in bladders as he was in musical theater.

I wanted to go to Princeton more than I had wanted anything in my life up to that point. I spent every non-application-focused moment poring over college admissions message boards, trying to calculate my odds of getting in based on the chatter of a hundred equally neurotic, type-A teenagers on CollegeConfidential.com.

I was up for anything that might give me an edge over my Internet chat room archnemesis: PrincetonGuy11. Anything to wipe that smug "double legacy" digital smile off his face.

When my mother told me that meeting and impressing a Princeton admissions officer named Mr. Bowman might give me that edge, my response was, "Great. Let's hunt him down," and I don't think I've ever seen her look more proud of me. According to a fellow mom she trusted, Mr. Bowman was a champion of arty candidates (like me), and Princeton had just received a $100 million grant for the arts, so he had more pull than ever in the decisions room. My mother translated this to: "If you meet and impress him you'll get in; if you don't, you'll end up at DeVry."

As soon as I was on board, she picked up the phone and dialed the number to Princeton's switchboard (from memory). She placed the call on speaker, so I could hear as well. Also, because cancer.

"Hello . . . yes, Mr. Bowman's office, please, in Admissions." She was using a beyond-unconvincing southern accent to disguise her voice. The Princeton switchboard operator, whom my mom spoke to roughly fifteen times a day, recognized her voice immediately.

"Oh, hi, Kim, let me transfer you." The phone clicked and began ringing, and my mother thickened her drawl.

"Hello, this is Mr. Bowman's office."

"Well, hi there, my name is Mrs. . . . Carpenheimer." First, *not* a real name. Perhaps it was a cross between her gastroenterologist, Dr. Oppenheimer, and just the word "carpet"? Either way, it was certainly not the name of a woman with the genteel southern accent my mother was affecting.

"Now, my daughter's applyin' for the class a 2011, and I'm a-wonderin' when that delightful Mr. Bowman's gonna be a gracin' the campus with his next admission information session?" And we suddenly shifted from Atlanta high society to a banana-mash distillery in the Appalachian Mountains.

The plan was to schedule our annual New York family trip to coincide with his schedule and wrangle a meeting with him at Princeton. I'm not sure how we would have done this, as admissions officers aren't supposed to meet with prospective students one-on-one, but I'm pretty sure my mother would have faked a heart attack if it meant alone time for us in the ambulance with him.

"Oh, this time of year, Mr. Bowman is only hosting admission information sessions in the South, Mrs. . . . Carpenheimer, is it?"

I couldn't help but feel a pang of disappointment. I could rationally see that meeting Mr. Bowman probably wouldn't make or break my entire application, but I was like an addict, and good news about Princeton was my crack. Any setback, no matter how minor, was crushing.

"Yes, yes that's right, Carpenheimer. I see. Well, can you at least tell me when he'll be returning?" My mother's accent slipped back to her native "Jersey Girl" as her frustration mounted.

"I'm sorry, ma'am, I can't. And he's going on a much deserved vacation as soon as he finishes this tour."

"Oh really?!" My mom perked up, and I prayed she wouldn't actually say what I thought she might. "Well, where is he going to be vacationing?!" Of course she said it. The conversation pretty much ended there. She shrugged as she hung up, "Well, it looks like we're headed south!"

We turned back to the Princeton website to research Mr. Bowman's schedule of southern information sessions. The only one that worked with our budget was in Virginia. Two weeks later we used all our miles and were on the cheapest plane my mother could find. She called the hotel the day before the admissions event to confirm his travel plans, pretending to be Mrs. Bowman.* So, we knew he would walk into the hotel at some point on the day of the information session. Unfortunately, we did not know *when* that would be. What this meant was that my mother and I would need to camp out in the lobby all day if we wanted to intercept him and sneak in a private conversation. Naturally, we did.

After a miserable red-eye flight, we walked into the lobby of a Courtyard Marriott hotel in Virginia at 8 a.m.

* Mrs. Bowman's voice sounded suspiciously similar to Mrs. Carpenheimer's.

on the big day. The well-trained front-desk clerk rose from his seat and asked us if he could help us check in. In an unbeatably sneaky move, my mother told him we were meeting an old friend of hers from high school. When he politely asked, "Oh, where did you go to high school?" she said, "South." Just the word "South." *So smooth.* After a few hours in the lobby, I'm pretty sure he thought we were a mother-daughter call-girl team looking for johns. I felt like Julia Roberts in the lesser-known classic *Neurotic Woman*.*

At 4 p.m., a man wearing an orange-and-black tie (Princeton's school colors) walked through the front doors. Showtime! My mother and I looked at each other, steeling ourselves for what would be the performance of a lifetime. You think Lady Macbeth is a challenging role? Try feigning surprise after you have traveled 3,000 miles and just spent eight butt-numbing hours on a plywood bench listening to a loop of torturous lobby music. We were ready, though. I had my entire résumé memorized as dialogue, and my mom

* That movie actually starred Julie Rabinowitz.

had her scripted "spontaneous" interjections down pat. I channeled Meryl Streep, and we approached him casually.

"Excuse me, Mr. Bowman?!"

"Yes . . . ?" He turned toward us. He looked exactly like the photos from all the internet stalking we had done—classic Northeast Ivy Leaguer: khakis, blazer with leather elbow patches, and of course, a fun tie to pull the look together.

"This is such a crazy coincidence!" I laughed with my carefully cultivated "surprised delight" giggle. "I'm Kate Siegel. We met at an information session at Princeton a few months ago; you probably don't remember me." I knew for a fact that he did not remember me, because while it was true that I attended an information session, Mr. Bowman was not the admissions officer who hosted it. "I'm applying next year. This is my mom, Kim. We're from California, but we're in Virginia for a family bat mitzvah! And I just love coming back here, because this is where I won my national speaking competition. What are you doing here?" *Résumé bullet point one, check!*

I paused as rehearsed, waiting for him to ask me about my speech contest, but also entirely prepared to humble brag unprompted.

"I'm here to host an information session. What a happy coincidence. And whose bat mitzvah? Mazel Tov!"

I froze. I couldn't remember my line! Well, technically, I hadn't rehearsed an appropriate line; in all our résumé prep, we hadn't cast a bat mitzvah alibi relative. Sensing that I was choking, my mother improvised.

"Thank you for the Mazels! Her baby cousin Jamie Schwartz is becoming a woman! By the way, Kate doesn't like to brag, but I'm the mom. That speech competition was a big deal. She won a big scholarship." We were back on script, and the act continued flawlessly.

I asked all my carefully rehearsed questions about the theater department, subtly slipping in the impressive artistic elements of my résumé. Each query struck the perfect balance: bragging as much as humanly possible about my accomplishments while still being vaguely reminiscent of a question about the school. My forgotten line was a distant memory, and our play was going better than I hoped. At the last second, my mother decided to veer off script:

"Are you headed back to Princeton tomorrow? We're driving up to New York, so we'd be happy to give you a ride. Princeton's on the way! It'd be easy!"

It would not be easy. In fact, if he accepted my mother's offer, we would need to cancel our flight and stay overnight. That aside, what on earth would I talk to this man about for a full four hours? I had nothing left! I blew my entire résumé in this conversation! Even worse, what would my *mother* say? As he tilted his head, I saw my entire high school career flash before my eyes, my chance at Princeton slipping away in this tacky hotel lobby. Curse you, Mother, you greedy, greedy beast. I held my breath.

"That's very kind of you, but I have a rental car." Thank God for Avis.

The whole encounter was maybe five minutes long, but my mother maintains to this day that this conversation was the reason I got into Princeton.

All things considered, I got off easy. If this were a Teeny Tiny Tim story, Tim and Ethel would have slashed Mr. Bowman's rental car tires in the night and embarked on a fabulous road trip from Virginia to Princeton, during which Tim would write a Tony-nominated play, discover a cure for cancer, and also get a handwritten letter of acceptance to Princeton's class of 2011.

1:20 am

< Messages **Mother** Details

@CrazyJewishMom

Remember those Vagina Steams I saw on goop? Changed my mind, I want to try one. Just heard it's a Mayan ancient healing practice. Want to go with me to get our vajayjays steamed?

Um...NO

Why not? Gwyneth Paltrow swears by them

Our vaginas do not need to be steamed

Please don't speak on behalf of my vajayjay. She wants a steam. And I'm taking her.

# Dr. Who (Ha)

My mother is the human version of WebMD. It's actually impressive. After talking to her for five minutes, you'll be convinced that even the smallest ailment is cancer or the black lung. "Oh, you have a zit? Well, I read a study that adult-onset acne can be a sign of polycystic ovarian disease—when was the last time you went to the gyno?" If I have a sore throat and make the mistake of mentioning it to my mother. "KATE, YOU COULD HAVE MENINGITIS!! TOUCH YOUR CHIN TO YOUR NECK!! DID YOU TRY IT? CAN YOU TOUCH YOUR CHIN TO YOUR NECK?!" Throw a few swollen glands in the mix, and you're definitely looking at Ebola.

Although where perceived illnesses are concerned, there is nowhere my mom's hypervigilance is more ferocious or disgusting than sexually transmitted diseases. The number of times she has shown me vile images of pus-filled genital warts and infected herpes sores is easily in the thousands. In high school it got to the point where I could have legitimately worked as an STD diagnostician. I could spot pubic lice in my sleep.

Between my headgear and the dancing crabs in my dreams, birth control and STD prevention weren't really things that needed to be discussed while I was in high school, but during the summer before my first year of college, my mom decided it was time for me to get fitted for a diaphragm.

I will never understand why my mother's preferred method of birth control was (and still is), of all things, the diaphragm. *You know what would make all this steamy sex we're having even hotter? A spermicidal-gel-reapplication break! Bust out that preloaded vagina jelly stick and get over here, sexy.*

She scheduled an appointment with a New York–based gynecologist before school started, so I would have a "lady bits" doctor close to campus.

"You need to be prepared, Kate. You're gorgeous; those horny college boys are going to be all over you.

FRESH MEAT! Mind you, this isn't the all-clear to start humping every guy on campus the second you get to school . . ."

In light of the chorus line of genital warts I imagined prancing around under the boxers of every man I saw, humping frat guys was not at the top of my college to-do list. That said, I had yet to French-kiss a boy, and I was extraordinarily sexually frustrated. It was getting to the point where I would catch myself fantasizing about dry humping strangers in the street after making brief eye contact. Oh, if the Westwood Subway sandwich chef only knew the things I imagined doing with him on top of the vegetarian-topping trays.

It was a confusing time, so I'll admit, getting birth control was probably wise. Besides, all the television shows and movies I'd watched suggested that college was a sexy time of experimentation and freedom, even for late bloomers like me.

We arrived in New York a few weeks before classes started to shop for dorm accessories and visit my aunt on the Upper West Side. On the afternoon of the doctor's appointment, after hours of arguing about hampers in a nightmarishly vast Bed Bath & Beyond in Manhattan, we made our way over to my new gyno's office.

Of course my mother insisted on staying in the exam room with me, and we waited together for the doctor. I was crinkling my paper gown nervously, my legs dangling over the edge, firmly closed. My mom gestured toward the stirrups.

"What're you waiting for? Spread 'em!"

"No!"

"Oh, come on! What're you, shy all of a sudden?"

The examination room was lit with unflattering fluorescent panels that simultaneously made my acne and budding frown lines more pronounced. I worried that in this light my cobweb-dusted vagina was not being set up for a good first impression with Dr. Weiner. A disembodied model of the female pelvis was resting on the counter of the cabinet-and-sink unit to my right. The three-dimensional anatomical sculpture was spliced down the middle, exposing the intricacies of a healthy female reproductive system. To me, it was just a blank canvas on which to paint the horrors of sexually transmitted diseases. I named her Gonorrhea Gloria and was in the midst of imagining a particularly gruesome genital warts outbreak on the model's cervix when Dr. Sabrina Weiner walked into the room.

"Hi, Kate! Nice to meet you! What brings you in today?" She looked about forty, and she was wearing a cream blouse and high-waisted blue pants that were more "fashion girl" cool than "mom jeans" frumpy. A smart white lab coat, with her name embroidered in navy, pulled the ensemble together nicely. This intimidatingly chic woman just renewed my concern about my vagina coming off poorly. Can a lady get some mood lighting up in here? Honestly, she looked nice enough, but it's hard to get excited about someone when you know that the plan is for her to insert foreign objects into your vaginal canal. My mother chimed in on my behalf.

"Hi, Dr. Weiner! So, Kate will be starting college—PRINCETON—in a few weeks, so we wanted to get her fitted for a diaphragm and talk to you about sex."

I blushed about the fact that my mother felt the

need to scream "Princeton" everywhere she went since the day I had gotten in to the school.

"Princeton! How impressive! Well, you have a very responsible mom, Kate. Are you sexually active?"

"Nope, not a man in sight." my mother responded enthusiastically.

"No. Not yet," I confirmed.

"All right, can I have you swing your legs up onto the table and scootch your bottom all the way down to the edge and put your feet in the stirrups?"

I complied, pulling at the paper gown as I placed my legs into a spread-eagle position. *Here we go, vagina, time to sparkle, baby!*

"Perfect. All right, honey, so I'm just going to do a basic exam here, and take a few measurements to get you fitted for this diaphragm. And we can talk about other birth control options as well."

Dr. Weiner removed her wedding ring, placing it on top of Gonorrhea Gloria, and applied plastic gloves. She smiled at me reassuringly and sat down on the little rolling stool between my legs, lifting up the thin waxy gown and revealing my vagina to the room. She didn't recoil, so that was good, but I could feel Gloria judging the shit out of me.

"Okay, so you're going to feel some pressure." She inserted a finger, and I squirmed uncomfortably. "No, no, don't clench, honey. Try and just relax. Breathe."

My mother was completely uninterested in the fact that a stranger's gloved finger was halfway up my hooha for the first time and took this as an opportunity to rehash the safe-sex lecture I had heard a thousand times over. "Now, Dr. Weiner, just so she hears it from a doctor too . . . can you back me up? College guys are some of the horniest, most disgusting herpes-riddled liars on the planet. And it's important to make them get tested for STDs before she decides to have sex, right?"

Dr. Weiner, who, just as a reminder, is wrist-deep in my vagina at this point, looked up at me.

"Well, I can't speak to the first part of that, but I do agree that it's very important to be safe, and a lot of girls feel intimidated about asking a guy to get tested."

*PUH-LEASE!* I smiled. STD testing was as integral to my sexual fantasies as moody music and chocolate-covered strawberries (my understanding of sex at that time was a mash-up of '90s romcom montages and Nora Roberts's futuristic mystery-romance novels). I glared at my mother.

"Well, you need to hear it from a professional too—you don't listen to me. NO STD TEST, YOU WON'T BE GETTING SEXED! Think about herpes, and HIV, and CRABS . . . Do you want me to show you the pictures again?"

Dr. Weiner smiled and looked up at me. "I think what your mother is trying to say is that it can be tricky sometimes when you're in the moment and a guy doesn't want to get tested. But if it's a guy worth your time, he will understand and be happy to respect what you want."

"Exactly!" My mother nodded emphatically as Dr. Weiner continued. "Sometimes you have to kiss a lot of frogs before you meet your prince."

"Yeah, and college man-children frogs have WARTS. Genital warts!"

"They can." Dr. Weiner smiled with her straight, blindingly white teeth, and I tried to imagine her kissing a genital-wart-ridden frog to make the situation less mortifying.

"Speaking of princes, where did you meet yours? Your ring is beautiful." My mother gestured toward the simple diamond engagement ring that was lying on top of Gloria.

"I met him in college."

"Oh, really? That's fabulous! What does he do?" Dr. Weiner removed the finger that had been rooting around my lady parts and reached for what looked like a medieval metal torture device, which, as it turned out, was just a speculum.

"Okay, honey, this is going to be a little more pressure." She pushed the cold device inside me and responded to my mother, "He's a theater producer."

My mother perked up in her seat and immediately sprang into Drone Mom mode. With college admissions behind us, she had already begun thinking about internships that would set me up for a career in the arts, though she was still campaigning for me to go to law school. This was the one and only subject that could have distracted her from the STD campaign of terror. I was grateful for Dr. Weiner's choice of husband and felt a pang of guilt about forcing her to kiss the genital-wart frog.

"Really? A producer? Kate's a very talented musical theater writer! She's a songwriter and performer too!"

Dr. Weiner looked up at me, still just fully immersed in my vagina. "Oh, really?"

My mother sat forward in her chair. "Kate, why don't you sing one of the songs from the musical you wrote?" If the speculum weren't halfway up my vagina, I would have leapt off the examination table and strangled her.

Dr. Weiner shifted the metal device. "No, no, honey, don't clench. Breathe."

Apparently I hold all my tension in my vagina. My mother charged ahead, speculum and swabs be damned! "Come on, Kate, sing 'Asian Boy's Lament' . . . Dr. Weiner will love it, and it'll relax you . . . relax your lady bits!"

Context: The musical I wrote in high school was about college admissions stereotypes, and one of the characters was called Asian Boy as part of the satire.

When I did not begin singing, she nudged my arm. "Come on!" And then she began belting out the lyrics to Asian Boy's big number, "Why Not A Plus?," in a horrifyingly over-the-top generic Asian accent.

"Mother, can you *not*?!"

Dr. Weiner stepped in on my behalf. "Okay, ladies. Maybe you'll sing it for me after? But right now, I need you to breathe and try to relax your muscles."

I glared at my mother once again, and she backed off but left my CD (she carried a copy with her wherever she went) with the doctor to give to her husband. We never heard from him, and when the time came? I opted for condoms.

4:05 am

< Messages **Mother** Details

@CrazyJewishMom

Kate

Kate

Kate

Text ur mother

Kate?

Kate

Kate

Kate

Answer ur cell

Call me

Call me

Kate

Kate

Okay

Ok I'm calling dad then police

# Do Not Open Unless You Want to Cry

When I was born, my mother forced anyone who entered our home to bathe in hand sanitizer and wear a hospital mask as soon as they walked through the door. She also hired a British nanny whom she then refused to let hold me or, for that matter, even touch me. One night during a dinner party, when my mother wouldn't hand me over to the nanny for a nap, a friend at the table jokingly defended my mom with: "Hey! If the nanny wants a baby . . . let her have her own fucking baby!"

Unfortunately, my mother adopted this sarcastic quip as a serious mantra and never let me out of her sight for the next eighteen years. Even in college, the helicoptering showed no signs of faltering.

During my freshman year, however, I was grateful to have her helping me navigate the minefield that is the life of a female college freshman. I think the best way to describe my first week on campus was that it felt like getting smacked in the face with a testosterone stick, and I called my mother every night for advice.

Realistically, I probably could have just met her for dinner at her hotel, as she hovered around campus for the first few weeks of school. There was a lot to discuss—it was a complete and utter shock for me to find that there were men who actively wanted to have sex with me. The great thing about Princeton was most of us were sexually frustrated nerds who spent high school working instead of socializing, so the alcohol flowed, and quoting Shakespeare was considered an acceptable come-on. That was great news for me. "This lady dothn't protest at all!"

In high school, I kissed boys during musicals and played Truth or Dare a few times, but I never had a boyfriend. Technically, any and all smooching I *had* done up to that point was either the result of someone being forced to kiss me in a school play or being compelled to by a party game.

Within a week, I fell in puppy love with a sophomore named Adam Reitner. I met Adam in the dining hall one day, and he told a friend of mine that he thought I was hot. So yeah, we were in love. He was sarcastic, tall, and Jewish—not a bad start for someone like me who has erotic fantasies about Larry David. I had also assigned Adam an enormous penis in my daydreams, which didn't hurt.

I wasn't sure when to expect the sex stuff to start happening, but we were spending a lot of time together, and I thought things were going well. I even bragged to my mother. *Remember how you thought I was going to die alone? Might not be the plan!*

"You know that guy Adam I told you about? We've been hanging out for like a few weeks . . ." Translation: We've been doing a lot of "group hangs," drinking, and sloppy inebriated dancing together while out partying.

"Do you have your diaphragm yet? Does it fit? Have you gotten Adam tested for STDs? You need to make sure you get the report directly from *his* doctor. You don't want some herpes-riddled liar conning you into sex and infecting you with vagina sores for the rest of your life."

"Oh my God, Mother! We haven't even kissed yet!"

"You've been dating for three weeks, and he hasn't kissed you yet? Is he gay?"

"NO! We're not like officially dating, we're just hanging out, and I know he's attracted to me, and I don't know! We're taking it slow!"

"Sounds gay."

When we hung up, I realized she did have a point. Why *hadn't* Adam made a move? Was it my back fat? I decided that I was going to have to make my intentions more plain and my control tops tighter. I had already been drunkenly pointing at him on dance floors and trying to corner him for make-out sessions in basements. Defining this ridiculous, one-sided mating ritual as "hanging out" stemmed from my complete and utter lack of relationship experience.

In my defense, though, it also came from watching my female peers "hang out" and tolerate barely human treatment from men who wanted to "keep things casual" and weren't "into labels." "Hanging out" encompasses a wide variety of sexual interactions, but it's really just the collegiate excuse to screw anyone you want with no strings attached. Have fun, kids!

How could I make things more mortifyingly obvious for Adam, you ask? By rubbing my ass against his crotch on dance floors, of course! When I tried this, he didn't even pop a boner, which was pretty routine in my admittedly limited experience. Though I suppose this makes sense in light of the forcible nature of my public dry humping.

Frustrated, I ignored all my mom's texts that night and went to bed. At 6 a.m., I woke up to two public safety officers pounding on my door. I assured them that I had not been kidnapped and called the woman who sent them.

"ARE YOU KIDDING ME, MOM!? You called campus police!?"

"Oh thank God you're okay! Why the hell didn't you respond to my texts?! I must have sent you fifty messages." Sixty-three, actually.

"I was busy!!!"

"Oooo-la-la! With Adam?! How'd it go last night?"

"Not well. He was so aloof!"

"GAY!"

"Come on, stop. I dunno, it's so confusing. We hang out all the time, and I think I'm being pretty obvious about liking him."

"Well, you've been all over him; why not try playing a little hard to get? Stick your tongue down another guy's throat and let him watch!"

This seemed like a reasonable idea, but the next day, I got some news from a mutual friend: Adam was already discreetly "hanging out" with someone else, and he had been since before I met him. I immediately dialed my mother and told her the news.

"Aw, I'm sorry, honey. But it's good to know now! There's so much gorgeous manmeat at Princeton. What about Tim? Now that's the kind of sperminator *I* went after in college! Big hunky wrestler guy."

"Mom! Tim's my resident advisor! It's like *illegal*! And what do you mean you're sorry? I think this is great about Adam!"

You would think I'd take this as the disappointing news that it was and move on to the next. Oh no! In my lust-riddled brain, I rationalized that Adam *truly* loved me but just couldn't bear to disappoint the girl he had met first.

"Honey, you can't be serious . . . ?"

But I was! You know, that classic love story:

Boy meets Girl One.

Boy has months of great sex with and is totally smitten with Girl One.

Boy frantically avoids sad advance after sad advance being made by Girl Two.

Boy secretly falls in love with Girl Two, while still maintaining all outward appearances of being super into and dating Girl One.

Boy marries Girl Two.

That was my five-year plan, and a few weeks later, I got news that made me want to dance like a girl in a tampon commercial—Adam had broken up with Girl One! To quote my mother, "Ovaries, start your engines!" My five-year plan had been given a dramatic shove into high gear, and I rejoiced while dialing my mom.

She warned me not to get my hopes up, but I was too busy thinking about what our kids would look like to listen.

"MOM, I'M GOING TO HAVE HIS BABIES! ARE YOU READY FOR GRANDCHILDREN?!"

"Spawn: number one, don't you ever joke about grandchildren with me again. Number two, slow down. Forget grandbabies—you need to get him to the health center and get him tested. You sleep with him, you sleep with every girl he's ever slept with! STD testing before sexting!!!"

I think she was unclear about the meaning of sexting at that point, but I got the message.

It was a Thursday, and we were all going out that evening. I had my legs and pubes waxed for the first time, so I would feel sexy for my big night! This did not turn out as well as expected. I looked like a prepubescent burn victim, and the irritation transformed my walk into a waddle. Let me tell you, nothing says sexy like limping around a dance floor and discreetly icing your crotch with cold beer.

My mom called me at around 11 p.m., and this time I answered in an effort to avoid another visit from campus police.

"Mom, I'm out. What do you want?!"

"How's it going with Adam?" she asked.

I paused before responding and glanced around the room. At that point, Adam was too preoccupied with another girl to even notice I was there.

"Mother, everything's fine, just leave me alone. And don't call the police. I'm alive!"

Just as I hung up and turned back around, I saw Adam lean in and kiss another girl on the dance floor. I was devastated, so I went home, got into the bed I'd gone to the trouble of making for Adam's benefit, and slapped a cold can of Fresca on my vagina.

When I woke up the next morning, I opened my laptop and drafted a borderline psychotic, truly humiliating love letter, declaring my feelings for him and asking him out. I sent it to my mom and called her.

"Hey, Mom."

"You sound upset! What happened last night? Did

someone try and slip something in your drink? DID SOMEONE TRY AND DATE-RAPE YOU?"

"No, no I'm fine. Can you proofread the email I just sent you?"

"Sure, hang on."

Now, I don't remember exactly what it said, but I do remember that while I was writing it, it dawned on me that this might actually be the greatest love letter ever written. Who's Shakespeare again? Oh, that guy who used to write sonnets in iambic pentameter before Kate Friedman-Siegel redefined the very essence of what it means to be in love?

My mother sighed into the phone. "Honey, please don't send this."

"Why? It's how I feel!"

"Kate, I know this is so hard, but sweetheart, you have to accept that he is just a friend. He doesn't feel that way about you . . . I'm so sorry, honey, but you have to trust me, please don't send that note!"

My eyes welled, but even in the emotional chaos of that moment, my mother's transformation from the acerbic, funny woman I was used to into Mother Superior from *The Sound of Music* worried me. Either she was gearing up for a sarcastic rendition of "How Do You Solve a Problem Like Maria?" or perhaps she knew something I didn't.

"Mom, I have to tell him how I feel. If I never try, how can I possibly ever feel okay about that?"

She paused for a long time. I have to admire this rare moment of restraint. After suffering through hundreds of hours of Adam-centric conversations, my response to me would have been: "Never try?! NEVER TRY?! Are you kidding me?!? You have done everything but present yourself naked, vagina first, in his extra-long twin-sized bed!" Which is an indicator that I'm probably not ready to be a parent just yet. It's also a testament to my mother's understanding that this was a mistake I needed to make.

"Mom?"

"Yes, honey; I'm here. I don't think you should send it, but if you do, PLEASE take out the line about 'a romance for the ages.'" *Fair.*

As soon as we hung up, I sent Adam the letter. It did not go well.

Adam was very sweet about it, as sweet as a nineteen-year-old boy can be, and he gently showed me back to my seat in the friend zone. I think his actual words were something to the effect of "I—uh, but we're friends!"

Over the course of the following year, I kept the letter in a password-protected folder on my desktop called "DO NOT OPEN UNLESS YOU WANT TO CRY." The folder also contained terrible, angsty short stories I had written and other emails that teenage Kate deemed worthy of her "emotions" folder. I'd peruse its contents while shamefully cry-singing along to Christina Aguilera's "Beautiful." Every time I tried to look at Adam's email, though, I had to close it; it was just too mortifying. But we have remained friends to this day, so it wasn't a total loss.

My mom could have stopped me that morning, and she knew it, just as she knew I was setting myself up for a humiliating rejection and a subsequent period of tortured songwriting and rocky-road-related weight gain. But she recognized that it was time to cut (a small section of the very much still attached) cord and let me get hurt. She would rip the genitals off a lion in hand-to-paw combat to protect me, so watching me suffer my first heartbreak was probably miserable for her. Lion testicles aside, my mother knew that letting me suffer was the only way to help me grow up: "Sometimes, you have to get your heart broken to find your way around the penis."*

* This is begging to be cross-stitched on a pillow.

< Messages

6:05 am
**Mother**
@CrazyJewishMom

Details

Happy Birthday, Spawn! Or as I like to say: Happy "day ur mother was cracked open like a coconut to give u life" day.

# Happy Birthday, Spawn!

Loud pounding and a brassy voice singing "Happy Birthday" catapulted me into consciousness and also a raging hangover. "Happy birthday to my tushy gii-iirl! Hap-py birth-day too-oo yoooouuu!" It sounded a lot like my mother.

I groped around for my alarm clock and squinted at its angry red display. Eight a.m. I was lying next to my crush, Jared. Beautiful Jared, with his toned albeit alarmingly short torso, and his tortured pseudo-intellectual angst at peace for a brief moment while he slept. We were in my college dorm room in New Jersey, I was fully clothed from the night before, and it was the morning of my twentieth birthday. And my mother had come twenty-five hundred miles from our home in Los Angeles to sing at my doorstep?

"My God! This lighting! I need Botox just to stand out here!"

Yep, definitely my mother.

*SHIT! SHIT! SHIT!*

Of course I had no business being shocked. My mom is the queen of the birthday surprise. I tried to shake Jared awake as her pounding continued. "Uh, just a second!"

After nineteen years of birthday bombshells, including one where a flower deliveryman handed me a bouquet of tulips before stripping down to a G-string and singing a sexed-up rendition of "Happy Birthday," I had become conditioned to exercise hypervigilance each year around the anniversary of my birth. When January 20 rolled around, I was on high alert: Is that a *real* mailman, or is he about to deliver a *special package*, courtesy of my mother? Is that bartender humming of her own free will, or is this the start of an elaborate birthday flash mob?

Given my mother's track record, you would think I could have predicted this visit, but this year she had outdone herself. January 20, 2009, was also Barack

Obama's inauguration day, and she had me fully convinced that she was in Washington, DC, to witness the historic event.

Hope! Change! Not for my mother. And she wasn't content to just *tell* me her plans. No, the woman sent me forged travel documents detailing her flight from LA to DC, and she complained about the obscene price of her fictitious hotel stay. The night before, she even sent me a picture of herself in front of the National Mall. Due to all the overwhelming evidence that she was safely ensconced in our nation's capital, watching President Obama make history, I lulled myself into a blissful little bubble of complacency and invited Jared to spend a night of strictly "above the waist" action in my bed.

"My God, Kate, what are you doing in there?" my mother yelled. "Open the door! I don't care if you're naked, just let me in! You know I've seen that tuchus doing just about everything!" My mother raised her voice. "I've seen it naked, farting, pooping! Remember at your second birthday party when you started screaming in front of everyone: 'POOPY'S COMIN' AND IT'S A BIG ONE' . . . ?"

"Mother! Shhh! Stop!" I roused Jared from the coma-esque state he had drunken himself into the night before and sprinted over to the door. She was impeccably dressed in all black.

"What are you doing here?!"

I smiled apologetically at my hallmate Nicole, who had emerged from her room three doors down, rubbing her sleep-crusted eyes.

"I thought the poop talk might get you to hustle! Now, get your butt in gear. I've got a *big* birthday surprise for you!" Of course she did. How could a cross-country early-morning serenade be the only shock of this day?

"We've got to hit the road right now." She glanced down at the clock on her phone. "And I have to say, this is by far the best birthday gift I have ever given you!"

This was an unsettling thing to hear, as she used the exact same words to describe my 2007 present: a consultation with LA's top nose job doctor "in case you want to fix your nose before you go off to college!" *I didn't.*

"Move!" She brushed me aside, picking up a shirt

off the floor. "And of course it's a total wreck in here! We should have never cleaned up after you when you were growing up. You never learned to keep a clean hou—"

She trailed off as she rounded the corner and noticed Jared sitting at my desk, helplessly swaddled in a pale yellow blanket from the waist down, covering his bottom half. He had searched in vain for his pants, which were likely hiding in whatever recess of the room also contained my dignity.

"Well, well, well," my mother said. "Who is this . . . handsome young man?"

"Uh, this is Jared! We're just getting an early start on a project for playwriting. I thought you were in DC, Mom!" I stepped between them.

"Surprise!" She tilted her head. "Jared? I've never heard anything about a Jared!"

Nope! Not true. She knew everything there was to know about Jared. The unfortunate consequence of our extremely close relationship in this case was that I had armed her with the knowledge that Jared was a "player" who constantly pressured me to have sex. She hated him, and her advice to me from the first day I kissed him was "RUN!" In college, however, I realized a beautiful new freedom: the ability to filter my mother's advice. I could send her calls to voice mail! The twenty-five-hundred-mile divide gave me the flexibility to choose which of her suggestions (demands) to heed.

Now, the physical buffer between my mother and my questionable decisions had collapsed, and here she was, rifling through my belongings and approaching Jared like a lioness stalking her prey. But Jared just sat there, blissfully unaware of the tsunami about to crash over his artfully faux-hawked hipster little head.

"Uh. Hi, Mrs. Siegel . . ."

"It's Friedman, Kim Friedman, but you can call me Kim. So, how long have you two been an item?" First shot fired. She knew that Jared and I were not "an item."

I had once mustered the courage to ask him about being exclusive, and he led with "Monogamy is such a bougie construct," followed that up with, "I just got out of a relationship" (he hadn't), and closed with, "Let's just keep things chill."

Maybe I should have seen that coming. This was a guy who constantly tried to have anal sex with me, arguing: "Just let me put it in your butt; you'll still be a virgin. God, are you really going to give me blue balls again?"

I always felt guilty when he said things like that, which is absolute bullshit. For anyone unfamiliar with the term, "blue balls" refers to the *slight* discomfort *some* men feel when they've been aroused for an extended period of time without ejaculating.

"Frankly, I don't care if it feels like an elephant is stomping on your testes; your arousal does not entitle you to any of my holes or appendages. You're lucky to be in my bed, so shut the fuck up and masturbate forth!" . . . is what I should have said. Sadly, I always just blushed and apologized. My mother's anger toward him smoldered hotter with each day our casual arrangement continued.

Now, you might be wondering why *I* was willing to tolerate that kind of treatment. College had worn me down. It was my second year at school, I had yet to nab my first boyfriend, and I wanted to fall in love. Every guy I made out with on the dance floor only wanted a single serving from the Spanx-sponsored buffet I offered up each weekend, so the fact that Jared was coming back for seconds made me feel like Helen of Troy/ Beyoncé!

"You know," I said, "Jared probably has to go now." I stepped closer to the desk where he sat.

My mother rolled her eyes with such gusto, it's a miracle she didn't detach a retina. She threw my own words right back in my face.

"Where does he have to go? You two are working on your project, *right*?"

She didn't wait for a response, whipping toward me, her nostrils flaring wide. Her eyes darted around the room, and I could tell the focus had shifted from Jared to a new outrage.

"Kate, what is that smell? I smell pee! Oh, for the love of God, tell me you didn't get a cat! We talked about this, Kate! No more animals!"

"No, no, no, I didn't get a cat, Mom."

At this point I should probably mention that the reason my mother smelled urine was because Jared had wet the bed and thrown his pants off in his drunken stupor the night before.

"A DOG?! Kate, you agreed when you went away to college, you promised that there would be no more animals! Your father and I are not taking care of any more of your rescues!"

I'd like to take a moment to object to my mother laying the blame on me for the fact that we have five dogs, two cats, and three fish. She is responsible for ownership of at least 70 percent of our pets.

"No, Mother, I don't smell anything . . ." She kept scanning the room as I tried to think of a reasonable excuse. "But they were just . . . uh, spraying for pests downstairs so maybe that's why you smell someth—" I knew as soon as the words came out of my mouth that this was the wrong thing to say.

"What?! They sprayed for bugs!? I'm getting a hotel room for you right now; get your things!"

All thoughts of Jared had been abandoned for a far more pressing concern: cancer. Pest exterminators are very high on my mother's list of carcinogenic threats.

"Mother, it's fine. I'm actually not even sure if they

spray—" I tried to backpedal, but she wasn't listening to me.

"Are you kidding me?" my mother interrupted. "Breathing even one ounce of that stuff is like inhaling ten pounds of asbestos!" *Not scientifically accurate.* "No, no, my daughter is not getting your cancer, thank you very much, Princeton! I'm calling the housing department; this is outrageous! Why don't they just hand out cancer lollipops at orientation! Maybe they should start serving cancer juice next to the orange juice in the cafeteria!"

Then, in what seemed to me like slow motion, she turned around to my bed and pulled down the covers: "Come on, let's strip your linens and get your laundry done, you're not staying here anyw—" She trailed off as she came face-to-face with the enormous round wet spot in the middle of the bed and Jared's wet pants tangled in the sheets.

"Noooo!" Jared reflexively sprang upright, beet red, and the blanket covering his naked legs fell to the ground.

My mother heaved a great sigh that was 50 percent

disgust and probably 50 percent relief that the reason she smelled urine was not the result of a brain tumor pressing on her olfactory cortex (a fear that undoubtedly crossed her mind). She glanced at Jared from across the room; he was wearing only soggy boxers from the waist down. Smiling like someone had just handed her a winning Powerball ticket, she started stripping the linens while Jared pulled the blanket back around his hips.

"Oh, you shouldn't be embarrassed by this, Jared," my mother said sweetly. "It happens to a lot of men, especially when they drink. I read an article on AOL the other day about adult-onset bed-wetting, and it said it can happen because of stress, you poor thing." If the cause of the bed-wetting hadn't been stress before, it certainly would be now.

"But it can also be a sign of prostate cancer," she continued, "so you really must go see a doctor. When was the last time you had your prostate checked?" Now she was just having fun.

"I—uh . . ." Jared was deflated.

"You can't remember?! Oh, well, then you better go

to the doctor to take the test; it's easy! They just pop a couple fingers up your tush, poke around, and cough cough you're done!"

"Mother! Stop!"

She gave me an icy look that in the language of Kim Friedman stares translates to *I know exactly what I'm doing; you're lucky I'm not murdering this fool with my bare hands* and forged ahead, all smiles.

"Well, in either case, you must immediately start doing Kegels. They can help increase your bladder control."

"I—uh . . ." Jared mumbled. His words were barely audible, and it looked like he might collapse into the fetal position.

"What? It works!" my mother said. "Jared, I'm telling you. Kate and I do them all the time. Men can do them too! Come on, it's easy. Just clench. See, I'm doing them right now!"

"Okay, thanks, Mrs. Friedman." My mother waved jovially as Jared rushed toward the door, clutching the blanket around his hips.

"Bye, Jared!" my mother said. "Are you sure you

don't want to borrow some of Kate's jeans? It looks like you're the same size!"

Jared practically sprinted out of my room. The door swung shut, and my mother turned and gave me a pointed look.

"Well, you sure know how to pick 'em!"

"Mom, I can't believe you! Did you really have to do that?" I collapsed against the wall, in the grips of an agonizing hangover.

She paused from stripping the bed and lifted the urine-soaked sheet for effect. "You can't believe *me*?" she asked. "Well, I guess it didn't occur to me that I might offend the delicate sensibilities of a drunk bed wetter with a little Kegel talk!"

I clutched my throbbing forehead. "Mother . . ."

She steamrolled through. "How could you possibly be interested in him?!"

I responded with the ugliest cry of my life. I'm never the girl with a single glistening tear streaming down her perfectly made-up face. On this day, though, I was violently hung over, and I had opted for a dramatic smoky eye the night before.

Bravely, my mother dropped the linens to the floor and hugged me, pulling my twitching snot- and mascara-coated face onto her shoulder.

"Okay, okay. I'm sorry, honey," she murmured into my ear. "I just couldn't help myself. The guy's a nightmare." She hugged me.

I wasn't crying because she had embarrassed me (though she had); I was upset because she was right. Jared treated me like crap, and I tolerated it because I was lonely. I was so grateful that in that moment I was not alone, lying in the urine-soaked bed I had made for myself. Of course I would never admit any of that to my mother!

"Jesus, Mom! You seriously just ruined everything! He was about to ask me to be his girlfriend!" Clearly not, but I wanted to twist the knife.

"Okay, I'm sorry. I love you."

I inhaled a deep shaky breath.

"Come on, let me make it up to you. We've gotta go. You're going to *LOVE* your birthday present!"

---

Two hours later, I stood shakily in the door of a South Jersey beach house, as my mother beamed at me expectantly.

Was this the site of a sneak-attack surprise party? Were all my friends about to emerge from their hiding places?

My mother folded her arms impatiently. "Well? What do you think?!"

I looked around, confused. "Um, about the house? It's lovely. Who lives here? Also, can I use the bathroom?" A fresh wave of hangover-related nausea coursed through my body.

"WE DO! We bought it, and we're moving from Los Angeles to be close to you! Your father, Roxy, Bella, Murphy, Thor, Mooey Louie, Lola, and Ozzycat! And the fish! Happy birthday!"

I stood there for a moment, stunned.

"Well!?" my mother prompted.

And then I threw up.

8:18 am

< Messages **Mother** Details

@CrazyJewishMom

"Twentysomethings who don't feel anxious and incompetent at work are usually overconfident or underemployed." —Meg Jay, The Defining Decade.

Keep writing, spawn. it's all going to be ok.

# Keeping Up with the Friedman-Siegels

On February 11, 2011, I was in a gay bar in rural New Jersey, standing next to my mother, while a lesbian stripper pulled down my shirt and tried to lick my nipple. How did we get here?

It all started in 1971 on Broadway in New York City. *Relax, the chapter is only twelve pages, I'm not going to take you through a comprehensive history of musical theater.* At the time, Joe Papp was one of the most important people in American theater, and during my mother's first year in the directing program at NYU-Tisch, she decided to write him a brassy, deeply personal letter. The note insisted that he hire her to direct a production of Shakespeare's *The Comedy of Errors,* and further, that her concept for the play would revolutionize theater. To recap, my mother told the man who was responsible for *Hair*, one of the most controversial, groundbreaking musicals in history, a man whose legacy has enabled five million people and counting to see brilliant, star-studded productions of Shakespeare's work for free in Central Park . . . she told this man that *she* was going to define his career.

In a move that I can only imagine came out of sheer curiosity as to what kind of raving lunatic would have the ovaries big enough to write him such a thing, Joe Papp called her. "Hi, is Kim Friedman there? It's Joseph Papp calling." Believing it was her best friend pulling a prank, my mother said the following words to a man who, again, is an American theatrical treasure: "FUCK YOU, RICHARD! YOU'RE NOT FUNNY! SO JUST GO FUCK YOURSELF, OKAY?!" And then she hung up.

Miraculously, Mr. Papp called back and eventually gave her a job. Not directing, of course; I believe the official job description read "Coffee Bitch." But fetching coffee and lemonade for the actors in his productions was her big break and led to a career of directing plays for Joe Papp at the Public Theater in New York. Unfortunately, the success of that letter taught my mother a dangerous lesson that would inform her behavior for years to come and eventually haunt her then unborn child. Put simply: It pays to take risks.

When it was time for me to start my career, my mom wanted me to apply this same principle that had worked so well for her when she was starting as a young professional in New York. I was too insecure to admit to her or to myself that I really wanted to write, so I was applying for tangential creative jobs in the entertainment industry. "You have to stop being so timid. You need to grab people's attention; they are sifting through thousands of résumés, and you need to stand out."

Some of her fantastic job-application ideas:

1. Stalking Lorne Michaels at his favorite restaurant in Manhattan.
2. Delivering my résumés in giant boxes filled with glitter to make them stand out.

3. My personal favorite: submitting "a musical résumé."*

While I'm fairly certain that hand delivering my application to a theater production company and then breaking out into *A Chorus Line*'s "I Hope I Get It!" in the lobby (another actual idea she proposed) would have stood out in the wrong way, she was right. The job market was terrible, and I was trying to break into the entertainment industry, where even unpaid internship positions have a 1 percent acceptance rate. The acceptance rate for Harvard University is 5.9 percent.

"Don't be so traditional! You're whining about how hard it is to get a job? Cry me a river! You think Mark Zuckerberg and Steve Jobs whined? No, they worked their butts off and made something HAPPEN!" Her point was that I should channel ole Zuck's entrepreneurial spirit and create my own job or, at the very least, do something so impressive that every employer would be clamoring to hire me. For an English major at

* No, she never clarified what that meant or how it would have worked.

a liberal arts college with essentially zero life skills, the question became: *how?*

I found my answer in the controversial reality television series *Jersey Shore. Naturally.* The show was on the air while I was in college, and I got my mother hooked on Snooki, JWoww, and the rest of the gang during my junior year. After one particularly insane episode, I texted my mom:

OMG, did you see last night's episode?

**I know. Snooki got punched in the face. I want to go castrate that asshole who hit her. Nobody touches my Snooks.**

Yeah, what a jackass. I don't know though, the show's amazing, but the frustrating thing is that there's no sexual diversity. It's a bit heteronormative, don't you think?

I was neck deep in gender studies at that point.

Did u really just use the word heteronormative, Madame English Major?! I want to punch u in the turtleneck when u talk like that.

Whatever. I'm just saying, would a few characters to represent the LGBTQIA community kill them?

And this was the conversation that spawned my *Gay Jersey Shore* idea. *I may not know how to balance a checkbook, but I can operate a video camera!* The plan during my senior year became: "I'll create my own reality show, it'll OF COURSE get on TV, and then I'll either have my own production company or other companies begging me to come work for them!" My mother was thrilled with my delusional plan.

While the notion of starting a company and impressing potential employers with a professional industry credit are theoretically great ideas, there were a few major flaws with my master plan:

1. It is very hard to sell a TV show.
2. This concept, the name of which we changed from *Gay Jersey Shore* to *Under the Rainbow* to make it more "original," was, at best, a blatant rip-off. And it was a rip-off of a show already taking heavy fire for being exploitative and promoting negative stereotypes of everything from women to Italian Americans to the state of New Jersey. Just take that already troubled reality TV model, throw in an extremely polarizing demographic of the US population (the LGBTQIA community), and you've got yourself a controversy-free hit show!
3. Oh, and of course, there was my complete and utter lack of experience with reality television production.

My mother thought it was a "killer" idea, agreed to mentor me through the production elements, and jumped fully on board. I planned to find a bunch of sexually diverse youths with interesting stories, put them together in a house, let the cameras roll, and then cut together a flashy sizzle reel of characters to sell as a TV show. With no budget, the house in which we would ultimately film several weeks' worth of utterly insane footage would be ours! My mom, our producing partner Lauren, and I operated the cameras, and my father cooked for the thirty reality-TV hopefuls running around our home. I'm 86 percent sure two strangers had sex in my bed and 100 percent certain that my father was propositioned by a gorgeous transgender woman who loved his (admittedly fantastic) chicken wing recipe.

Long before our house could become a reality TV sex den, I had to organize a casting call to find our stars. My mother's professional directing credits, combined with the fact that the idea of doing a gay rip-off of *Jersey Shore* was an understandably controversial concept, resulted in several write-ups about our upcoming auditions in local Jersey and Philly publications. In my mind, I was already nominated for an Emmy. Move over *Hoop Dreams*, here comes *Gay Jersey Shore*!

Honestly, the intent was never to exploit the LGBT community—from my perspective, it was shitty that the only gay characters on reality shows on mainstream television were either homosexual or lesbian (maybe bi), and the complex, diverse spectrum of sexuality was being overly simplified and underrepresented.

In retrospect, a party-centric, booze-fueled reality television show *may* not have been the proper vehicle for a nuanced exploration of human sexuality. And what network was this going to be on? Bravo? Can't you just hear Andy Cohen? "You love *The Real Housewives of New York*? Well, up next we have *The Real Lesbian Gay Bisexual Transgender Questioning Intersex Asexual Allies of Atlantic City*!"

That said, the local stories about the casting call generated a huge amount of interest, and we convinced several gay bars around New Jersey and Philly to host casting nights for us and even to promote the event with their customers.

On the day of our first casting session, my mother, our producing partner, my dad, and I arrived at a tiny gay bar in Hammonton, New Jersey, with a helium tank, cameras, and a dream. By 6 p.m. the line of hopefuls was two blocks long. By 9 p.m. there were so many people, it was becoming completely unmanageable, and we forced my dad (who was only there to help decorate) to work.

My poor father was tasked with completing a preliminary interview with candidates before they were sent in to talk to us on camera. His goal was to give us a little background going into the interviews. My shy dad was shouting the following questions over loud club music all night:

1. What is your name?
2. What is an interesting fact about you?
3. What is your sexual orientation? How do you identify?

While these questions seem innocuous enough, he was getting answers like:

1. My drag name or my real name? Whatever, I'll just tell you both: Daisy Chain, Denise and Carl Nelson.

2. I once did a performance art piece where I had sex on a rotating stage with three other men.
3. Well, I'm a transgender woman, but I LOVE my penis! I'm never giving it up. And my boyfriends love it too, 'cause I can turn around and fuck the shit out of them!

As you can imagine, the people who showed up for what was advertised in the press as a *Jersey Shore*–ish reality show casting call were a little bit wild. By the end of the night, I had been licked, my mother both gave and received a lap dance, and my father took part in a dance-off. Oh, and the police arrived at 2 a.m. to shut down the event. My first casting call was a success! Huzzah!

After weeks of filming strangers in our house, I was convinced I was the next Shonda Rhimes. I edited together a sizzle reel of all the characters we selected, and I managed to convince a real Hollywood agent to try to sell the project! I AM SHONDA RHIMES; HEAR ME ROAR!

Predictably though, the show did *not* sell, and I was back facing potential postgrad unemployment in New York.

Even though it didn't work out, I am grateful my mother encouraged me to try this. Putting together this project bolstered my entrepreneurial spirit and emphasized the value of taking risks, of having the courage to try things I believe in, no matter how slim the chances of success might seem.

Was it scary for my mother to write a brassy, deeply personal letter to an iconic theater producer? Absolutely. Was it terrifying as a senior in college to march into a fancy Hollywood agency and try to convince people to take my project seriously? You bet! But taking that leap, even though the show didn't sell, made me realize that failure wasn't the mortifying, apocalyptic disaster I had imagined it would be. It was sort of an "oh, that's it?" moment. Then bring it on! And on a practical level, the experience prepared me for a job I would later get at Condé Nast, producing digital video. Though no one ever tried to lick my nipple while I was shooting for *Teen Vogue*.

2:20 pm

< Messages **Mother** Details

@CrazyJewishMom

SPAWN OMG OMG OMG HOLY DIAMOND RING UR BOYFRIEND IS GOING TO PROPOSE THIS WEEKEND.

What? Did he talk to you?

Think about it! We met the parents, it's ur two year anniversary Friday, and he's visiting ur FAMILY IN NEW JERSEY. THIS IS IT.

1. he's coming to visit ME
2. please don't get excited about this. I'm 99.99% sure it's not happening.

Trust me. Leave ur barn door open cause ur boyfriend's about to BUY THE COW.

8:45 pm

< Messages **Mother** Details

@CrazyJewishMom

Mom mom mom OMG you were right!!! OMG OMG he proposed!!!

I KNEW IT!!!!!!!!!!!!!!!!!!

OPEN THOSE BARN DOORS WIDE!!!!!!!!

LET THE COWS ROAM FREE

Omg omg dad and I r on the way

. . . he proposed that we get dessert in addition to dinner.

I'm burning the barn down.

# Listen to Your Mother

Why buy the cow, when you can get the milk for free? This is one of my mother's favorite platitudes, and as you can see, she does some fairly impressive acrobatics with it. Incidentally, I've taken to referring to my vagina exclusively as "the barn door."

As a feminist, my mom doesn't actually regard me as chattel, existing in a society where my worth and destiny are determined by whom I marry and how I look. We're talking about a woman who marched in NOW's 1970 Women's Strike for Equality in New York, carrying a sign that read "Birth Control Pills For Men!" We're talking about one of the first successful female television directors to make it in what is still a male-dominated industry. A woman who, after being warned by her agent that she could never get a job directing an action movie, went into an interview with a male executive at Paramount Pictures and addressed the issue head-on: "Look, I know you think I can't direct action because I'm a woman and I don't have a penis . . . so I got one!" And then she slammed a giant, veiny, flesh-colored dildo onto his desk. *She didn't get the job.*

It's confusing to reconcile this dildo-wielding feminist with a woman who feels the need to provide her own daughter with retro advice like "There are no platonic relationships after the age of eighteen" and "Don't waste your most attractive, childbearing years on a guy who won't commit." I know she'd love to tell me to grow my pit and pubic hair long, that my physical appearance is not an important factor in my relationships and has no bearing whatsoever on my career. Sadly, she recognizes that this isn't the way the world currently works. She wants the best for me, and I know it kills her to give me advice that's at odds with her feminist core. But how do we Jews confront uncomfortable societal realities? With humor! And in my mother's case, a lot of cow metaphors and sperm-bank talk.

She generally has a lot to say about my life, but she

doesn't hold back at all when it comes to the men I'm dating. Her advice is never sugarcoated, and it often comes in rude, unpolished packages. Over the years, however, I've had to come to terms with the fact that she is usually right. And that is really fucking annoying.

This brings me to James, my first *real* boyfriend during that weird twilight zone between college and actual adulthood. Until James, "boy talk" with my mother was really just me complaining about some guy who wasn't interested, until she got bored and told me to go study. But my relationship with James wasn't fictional, so there was more to talk about. After a year together, out came the clichés: "Just remember to dress up nice! Enough with the sweatpants. Remember, men think with their penises. Trust me, I know a thing or two about penii!" *Gross.* "I'm just saying, it's been long enough! He's met the cow, sniffed the manure, and been guzzling that free milk like a dairy farmer!" *Okay, so maybe not the exact clichés.* I rolled my eyes and dismissed her as old-fashioned. Plus, she just didn't *get* it. James and I were in love!

About two and a half years into our relationship, a

major hurricane swept through the Northeast. There was widespread concern that the city might lose water and power. As self-appointed Lord of the Neuroses, I sprinted to the grocery store for postapocalyptic hurricane supplies. James called me as I was stacking my cart high with bottled water and canned goods.

"Kate? Yo! I'm at the office; about to bounce, this shit is CRAZY! Just talked to my boy Nikhil, and the guys want to get lit tonight." Please note: James is a nerdy white male of Scottish descent.

"Okay, that sounds fun! I'm at the market now. I'll get extra food and stop by the liquor store. It'll be fun! I'll bring everything to your apartment."

"Sweet! See you soon. HURRICANE PARTAYYY!"

In my early twenties, a devastating natural disaster barreling toward New York seemed like a very convenient excuse to get wasted. I was also still in that post-college-love-affair-with-adulthood phase: good-bye Solo cups, hello stemless wineglasses! Farewell cafeteria, hello full kitchen! I've since reconsidered this enthusiasm for cooking and am now a loyal customer of takeout and my current boyfriend's ninja culinary skills.

That day, I decided I was going to be the perfect Hurricane Party hostess. I arrived at James's apartment and started mixing up alcoholic hurricanes and whipping together a dinner party (*so adult!*). I was slicing tomatoes when James arrived.

"Yo, babe, this is so weird. Bita just texted me."

I sliced a little more savagely. I had always been uncomfortable with his midthirties female colleague who would message him and email him outside of work. Whenever I asked him about her, he would always say, "*Dude, are you joking? I'm twenty-three! She's like forty! I work with her! You're being crazy!*"

"Oh yeah? What did she want?" I set the knife down.

"This is so weird. But I think she's hinting that she wants to come over." He was borderline giggling.

"Um, okay, did you invite her?" I folded my arms.

"No, I mean, I don't know! Maybe it would be good for my career, but this is so weird. She's like forty!

Why the hell does she want to hang out with a bunch of twenty-three-year-olds?" He broke off into another nervous giggle. The sheer amount of giggling should have been a red flag.

"Okay, so what do you want to do? That's so weird. Are you sure she's not into you?"

"Kate, stop being crazy!" There they were again, the most patronizing words on the planet. "She's just my work friend."

"Well, I don't know." I handed him a hurricane.

"Thanks. I think I should invite her. It'll be good. If she likes me, that could be *huge* at the office. She's so senior." What am I supposed to say to that? No? Let me just lift a leg and piss all over your career prospects?

"Okay."

James's two nerdy friends from college arrived, and we began drinking, drinking like we were infected with a fast-acting zombie virus and vodka was the only antidote. Bita arrived late. I was a bit cool to her at first, but then she complimented my bruschetta, and also there was alcohol, so we got friendly. I even texted my mother a smug message from the bathroom.

Guess who's here!

Who? Did u pick up drinking water? I read that the city may lose running water!

Yes, yes. That woman he works with, Bita. SEE! And everything's cool. She's actually really nice!

Yeah. Real nice until u find her with her hand down his pants!

Oh, stop. Seriously, he wasn't lying, she's a lot older than us. There's no way she'd want to date a twenty-three-year-old.

Who cares if she's older?! That just means the geriatric bitch might break a hip while she humps him.

Enough, Mother.

Whatever u say, spawn! Fill up ur bathtub, I've never seen a storm this bad. It's dangerous; there's going to be massive flooding.

After several rounds of shots and platters of food, James hopped up from the couch. "All right, we're doing it! WE'RE GOING OUT IN THE STORM!!!!!"

Now, you might be thinking, *That's crazy. Who decides they want to go outside in the middle of a Category 3 hurricane?* Because that is absolutely what I was thinking. Even though I had an alcohol blanket keeping me warm and dulling the natural fear responses in my brain, I distinctly remember thinking: *Hell, no.* I helped James into his jacket. His two gawky friends were chatting with Bita down the hall in front of the elevator.

"Be careful. Do you seriously want to go out in this?" I gestured toward a window back inside the apartment—wind and sheets of rain were unloading on the city. "Maybe you and I can just hang out?" I smiled at him flirtatiously.

"I'll be back in like fifteen minutes. I can't just let them go out alone—these are my *boys*, yo!" Again, he is a white Anglican male, and his "boys" are two gawky Indian guys with poor social skills.

"Okay. Love you." I shrugged.

"Later, babe!" He grinned and skipped toward the elevator. I turned back to the hurricane-like destruction in the apartment and began tossing empties into the trash and clearing plates. After forty-five minutes, I started to worry about his safety. I texted my mom.

Shit. James went out in the storm, and he's super drunk. I'm worried.

**What?! What the hell is he thinking? Are u serious? It's a HURRICANE.**

Yeah, I don't know. We're all really drunk. And they went out. Should I call the police?

**WAIT did he go out alone with the grandma who was at ur house??**

Well, they all went out together.

**Get the hell out there! Ur crazy to let that happen. I bet he's rolling her around into different walker-friendly sex positions right now. Ur crazy to let them alone together.**

You don't get it! You just don't know what it's like to have a real connection with someone, to TRUST! I trust him!!!! They're just friends!!!!"

**Kate, men and women can never be just friends.**

Oh, really? What's the plan? They're having sex on top of an abandoned hot dog cart on Seventh Avenue?

As it turned out, *kind of*. I later learned that James had been cheating on me with that woman and had fooled around with her that very night with a belly full of my bruschetta.

And there it was, my mother being proven right yet again, and the dark underbelly at the core of all her jokes peeking through, the truth on which all her relationship clichés are built.

While I don't agree with my mother's preferred method of ensuring faithfulness—locking your partner's package in a chastity belt—I was a bit too trusting and naive. Men are brought up in a system where ideas like "playing the field" and "keeping your bitch on a leash" are deserving of fist bumps and bro-y laughter. Meanwhile, women are asked, "Why are you acting so jealous?" and "Are you on your period?" I know my mom would like to dick-slap the face of every idiot who reinforces that kind of crap with her big fleshy dildo, but she's just trying her best to help me navigate a world where sexism is still very real. On paper, my ex looked great—well educated, good job, nice family. In reality: irritable bowel syndrome, anxiety disorder, cheater. In my experience, I've found that while there are certainly exceptions, my ex just happened to be the rule.

I guess the moral of the story is: Speak softly but carry a big dildo.

3:30 am

< Messages **Mother** Details

@CrazyJewishMom

OMG dad and I just saw the most amazing thing. It's a taser that takes a picture of who you shoot and it fits in your pocketbook. We're going to order you one for Hanukkah. What color do you want? Look out Mr. Rapist!

# The Castrator

If my mom were a superhero, her secret identity would be The Castrator—a television director and sassy mom by day, a defender of women and children by night. Her shape-shifting superpower would morph her into whatever form a sexual predator found most alluring, and then she'd use her superhuman strength to beat the living shit out of them. Her signature would be one blood-red nail that extended into a sharp blade that she'd use to castrate the rapists and child molesters she confronted.

Now, my mom is *not* a superhero and she has never castrated anyone (to my knowledge), but like a superhero, she has a dark origin story that informs her overwhelming concern for my personal safety.

She was ten years old when a man who lived in her apartment building tried to grope her in an elevator. My mother *being my mother*, and following my grandmother's advice, punched him in the testicles and screamed, "GET OFF ME RIGHT NOW!" before running out on the next floor.

Not to get all Freudian, but I think this experience was formative for her parenting style in one major way: it put her on the constant lookout for sexual predators.

The moment I emerged from her uterus, everyone became suspect. The male nurse in the delivery room who tried to bathe me was told: "BACK OFF! I'll do it myself." Mind you, at that point, my mother was still on the operating table being sewn together after a C-section. And it only got worse! My high school graduation present was a rape whistle. By the time I went away to college, she was sending me rape sirens.

When I moved to New York after school, my mother's central means of protecting me became personal safety devices: Kubotans, knives disguised as combs, hot-pink canisters of pepper spray. You name it, she's given it to me and demanded that I carry it in my purse. In her defense, I once had a chilling experience walking from the subway to my apartment. A tremendously drunk man shouted at me: "I'm going to fuck you in your mouth, bitch!" When I didn't immediately report for fellatio duty, he threw a beer can at me. Again, he was very drunk, so the can hit a mailbox about three feet to my left.

As satisfying as it would have been to watch that particular man writhing around in Mace-addled agony, if I carried her weapons with me all the time, I would almost definitely go to jail for assault. While I don't support my mother's belief that the punishment for all rapists and pedophiles in this country should be public castration in Times Square, followed by forcing the criminal to eat his own testicles, I still get pretty worked up about the catcalling and casual sexual harassment that I'm conditioned to silently tolerate as a woman. While I'm quietly ignoring your "Smile, miss's," "Dammmn, girl's," and "Hey, sugar tits, you wanna suck on something sweet's?" I'm also fantasizing about peeling back the skin of your penis with a rusty nail. So, (1) arming a person with that kind of stifled rage is probably not the best idea, and (2) I guess I'm turning into my mother a little bit.

Besides, the three neighborhoods where I have lived in New York have been perfectly safe. In spite of my mother's apparent belief that the New York State Department of Corrections' policy is to release all sexual predators directly into my apartment building, I have never felt truly threatened.

One weekend, my mother was visiting from New Jersey, and I took her out to lunch at a coffee shop. Between mouthfuls of kale and complaints about the hipsters serving her seltzer out of a mason jar, my mom asked, "So, where's the Mace I sent you?"

"Uh . . ." I looked down at my plate.

"Excuse me, I'd like to see that pink pepper spray I sent that you promised me you'd keep in your bag at all times."

"Mother, I'm not going to play this game with you. Stop. Eat your lunch."

"Do you mean to tell me that you're just walking around this city every single day without any way of protecting yourself?!"

"Shhh, Mother!" I glanced around the restaurant;

people were staring at us. She raised her voice and sat back, addressing the room.

"Why, you're worried your cool hipster coffee shop friends here will think you're *uncool* for carrying a weapon to defend yourself? You know what else is uncool?? RAPISTS!"

To avoid scenes like that going forward, I decided that every time she visited in the future, I would need to stuff one of the weapons in my bag. And it works. Whenever she walks into my apartment, the personal-safety spot check begins before I can even say hello. The first thing out of her mouth is always "Where is it?" On one of these visits a few years ago, I selected a Kubotan, which is a small baton that, when gripped, reinforces a punch. In some cases, these small sticks expand out into longer clubs, like the ones policemen carry.

"So let's see it! Open your bag." I had only removed this weapon from its packaging a few minutes before her arrival, unwilling to get caught empty-handed again. When she asked, I rolled my eyes with the confidence of the president of the National Rifle Association and pulled the weapon out of my purse.

"Good. I'd prefer the pepper spray, but that's better than nothing."

"See? I don't know why you keep asking me . . ." I smirked, satisfied.

"Okay, okay, I stand corrected."

"I mean, it's a little bit insulting. What do you think, I'm *lying* to you?"

I could tell she felt guilty, and I made a show of placing the Kubotan back into my purse.

I then promptly forgot about the weapon entirely. This happens almost every time she visits, and given how frequently we see each other, I'd calculate that there's a 60 percent chance I'm unknowingly armed at any given moment. It's a miracle I haven't unintentionally maced a friend or a baby or something. *I'm profoundly uncoordinated.*

However, there was one time I wished I had my mother's insane weapons with me: on a trip to Texas for work. My first night there I walked into a restaurant and ran right into a real-life cowboy. He was a perfect gentleman, but as he opened the door for me, his coat lifted to reveal the ornate pearl handle of a gun tucked into a holster on his belt. I was stunned. This was the first time I had ever seen a gun being carried by someone who wasn't a policeman. The fact that there was only a foot between me and a weapon that could blast a hole through my body resulted in some hefty pit stains. Again, this man was lovely; he even said, "I hope you enjoy your time in Texas, ma'am," but I was incredibly uncomfortable.

In Texas, people seemed to wear guns the way I wear Spanx—99 percent of the time they're hiding under my clothing, and I feel unsafe without them. The rest of that week I felt like I saw weapons every time a jacket swung back or a pant leg hiked up too high. Given my anxious disposition, I'm not sure how many of those were actual firearms versus actual belts and socks.

The next week I traveled to Dallas to visit one of my closest friends, Russell, whom I've known since I was seven years old. He moved to Dallas for a job with

Glenn Beck, the man deemed too crazy for *Fox News*, but I was in no position to complain. I was going to take full advantage of the free accommodations in a new city for a quick vacation. My last night there, we were feasting on takeout and arguing about gay marriage when I noticed a black case on the breakfast bar in his kitchen. I asked Russell what it was.

"Oh, that's my gun. I picked it up on the way home. Just got it cleaned. Thanks for reminding me; I need to put it in the safe."

"WHAT?! YOU BOUGHT A GUN?! ARE YOU FUCKING SERIOUS?!"

*Et tu, Brute!?!?!* He picked up the case and showed me his Glock 19, a black nine-millimeter semiautomatic weapon. I was stunned. This wasn't just a random cowboy in rural Texas, this was one of my best friends, whom I love and respect. For some reason, seeing Russell brandishing this weapon ignited a panic. *Guns and crazy people are everywhere!!! (Not you, Russ. I love you.)*

"I don't know why you're so surprised by this, Kate.

It's insane to me that you walk around New York with *nothing* to protect yourself."

I remember thinking: *Am I the only person on the planet without a weapon? Perhaps my mother was right. I mean, I'm not talking about going out and buying a bazooka, but maybe a lipstick shiv makes sense.*

The next morning I waited in the security line for my flight back to New York, contemplating whether I would actually be able to pull a weapon on someone, no matter what the circumstance. After unloading my bags onto the conveyor belt, I walked through the scanner. The TSA agent manning the machine flagged me for an additional pat-down because of my baggy sweatshirt. I was grateful my mother wasn't there to point out: *Well, if you had worn the little tight black dress, you wouldn't have a gloved hand halfway up your hooha! You should always dress up when you travel. You never know who you might meet!* The TSA employee in possession of that gloved hand gave me the all clear, and I turned toward the X-ray conveyor belt to pick up my laptop and bags. A frowning uniformed man was holding my belongings at the end of the X-ray belt, and as soon as I turned, he made eye contact with me and waved me toward him.

Again, my baseline level of anxiety is pretty high, so as soon as our eyes met, my heart rate spiked, and I imagined possible scenarios. *Had I forgotten to throw out the water bottle I had been sipping in the Uber? Had I left that weed Mark asked me to carry in my bag two months ago? Had someone planted a bomb in my purse without my knowledge—was I going to take the fall?!*

The TSA agent gestured toward my bags. "Are these your belongings?" I nodded, saliva pooling in my mouth. "I'm going to need to take a look inside this bag." He felt around the inside of my purse with latex-clad hands and pulled out the hot pink Kubotan that I had so smugly deposited there weeks before.

*SHIT!!!!!! How was I going to explain this? Oh no, sir, that's not mine. I just had to lie to my mother about carrying it! Mothers, am I right?*

"Oh wow. I'm so sorry about this, sir. I—I completely forgot that was in my purse."

"You *forgot* that you're carrying a weapon while going through airport security?"

"I honestly did. Again, I'm so sorry. This is so silly . . ."

"This is not a joke."

My neuroses took over, and I flashed-forward three days: me in a Texas women's correctional facility with a cowgirl prison wife named Peggy forcing me to brew toilet wine.

"I know, I can't believe this is happening. I really did forget it was in my purse. I even flew with it from New York on my way here, and I didn't realize." *Foot, meet mouth.*

"You realize you just admitted to a federal violation . . . ?" *Foot, meet large intestine.*

"No! I just meant that this is all a big mistake. I'm really so sorry about this. Is there any way you can just take the thing and I can go?"

"Well, we'll have to see. I've seen some of these extend out into clubs, and if it's that type of Kubotan, you're going to have to come with me." He fiddled with the hot-pink weapon and walked over to the other officers clustered around the X-ray machine to confer.

*Yep. Definitely going to jail. Would I even make a good prison wife? Shit, maybe I'd have better luck with the guards. Would that make me a rat? No, Peggy, I would never betray you, baby. I'll get you all of the prison cigarettes; just don't shiv me.*

The TSA agent who had detained me returned, clearing his throat and holding out the hot pink Kubotan.

"Ma'am, it is a serious offense to try and carry a concealed weapon on an aircraft."

"Yes, sir, again I'm incredibly sorry. It really was a mista—" He raised his other hand as my jailhouse fantasy escalated.

"Now, this doesn't extend into a club, but if it had, I would have had no choice but to detain you. Do you understand that?"

"Yes, sir." I nodded, grateful it hadn't been the pepper spray.

"We're going to let you go ahead and fly today, but we're confiscating this weapon. And don't let this ever happen again."

"I promise, sir. It won't." I swung my bags over my

shoulder and raced past one of the female TSA agents who looked remarkably like my prison wife, Peggy.

As I landed at JFK, I thought maybe this brush with Homeland Security would give my mother pause. Hell, maybe I could even convince her to stop sending me tampon knives (don't Google it). Perhaps this near-arrest would be the testicle to break the Castrator's blade. I powered on my phone, and my mom was already texting me.

**Omg!! I just parked the car and a man flashed me! He just casually pulled down his pants and his PENIS was swaying around!!!!**

OMG!!! Are you okay?!? That's so gross!

**Relax I'm fine! I just said "Oh do u want me to look? hang on . . . I need to put my reading glasses on."**

Nope.

12:19 pm

< Messages **Mother** Details

@CrazyJewishMom

OMG HURRICANE KATE IS A THING

What?

"Tropical storm KATE Strengthens Near the Bahamas."

Oh

A RARE PIC OF HURRICANE KATE AGE 5

# Hurricane Kim

My mother was once tear-gassed and arrested while trying to break into the Pentagon during a Vietnam War demonstration (like all moms do). In the sports arena where the protesters were being jailed, she met and began dating an undercover FBI agent who was trying to infiltrate her activist group (like all moms are part of). He was disguised as a hippie, and I'm sure he started off with every intention of being a model government official. After a year of dating my mother, he grew his hair long, denounced the war, and joined a commune.

I share this anecdote, not to shame an elite member of the law-enforcement community, but rather to illustrate how persuasive my mom can be and to assure him that he shouldn't feel bad. He really had no chance. My mother could convince a sorority girl to eat gluten. Mel Gibson to get circumcised. Bill Cosby to undergo voluntary chemical castration! I'm actually thinking of starting a support group for everyone who has been persuaded to do something by my mother. You know, the kind they form for people trying to leave a cult? I'll call it Kim's Klub!

I would obviously qualify for Kim's Klub membership, based on any number of the thousands of outlandish things my mother has convinced me to do over the years. Not the least of which includes the time I nearly got arrested for peeing beside her on a beach, instead of using the "dirty" public restroom ten feet from where we were squatting.

An interesting, relatively new addition to our little support group is a firefighter named Lenny, who qualified for Kim's Klub in the aftermath of Hurricane Sandy.

When the storm struck the Northeast, my mother worked herself into an apoplectic fit. She called me the morning after the hurricane passed and insisted I come home from New York immediately.

"Mom . . . Mom? Can you hear me? Please do not come get me! Everything is fine!"

"Oh really? You have food?"

"Two weeks' worth."

"And water?"

"Gallons."

"The toilets aren't working in your apartment. What're you, walking down fourteen flights of stairs every time you have to use the bathroom?"

"Um, no, I'm uh . . ." I cleared my throat.

"You . . . you're what?"

"I have . . . Hefty bags." I sighed, and she was silent for a brief moment.

"My daughter will not be shitting in a trash bag, thank you very much. Your father's on his way."

My dad, ever the dutiful husband, followed orders to reunite the family, drove to New York, and chauffeured me all the way back to our home in Jersey. When we were about ten minutes away, I turned on the local radio station to hear storm coverage. The soothing, deep voice of a disc jockey crackled through the speakers.

". . . we're back live, giving you up-to-the-minute coverage of Hurricane Sandy. And now we're going to take a call from a local woman. Jeff, do we have her on the line?" There was a brief pause. "Hello, is anyone there?"

"Hello? Hi!"

"Hi there! What's your name?"

"Hi, my name is Kim Friedman; I live in what is *APPARENTLY* an evacuation zone, and these state troopers are trying to sentence my five dogs, two cats, and three fish to death!"

"Holy shit, it's Mom!" I cranked up the volume. She sounded like Liam Neeson in *Taken 4*, ready to take on whatever and whoever might be foolish enough to stand between her and her furry children.

"Okay, slow down, can you tell us what happened?" the radio host asked evenly.

"I went out to get more dog food and flashlights, and no one stopped me; now they won't let me get back into my house! My dogs and cats are totally alone! They will die, and they won't even let me go pick them up! Besides, the storm's OVER! Why didn't they stop me when I left!?" You would think the major police barricade, concrete dividers, and fleet of police cars with flashing lights blocking the entrance to our neighborhood would have tipped her off, but no.

"Okay, where are you?" the announcer asked.

"I'm standing at the barricade. Please, anyone out there listening! Call the governor! Call the state police! Call me! These people are sentencing my precious babies to death! Call me at 609-555-7894! Please! Someone help us!" Yes, that was my mother, screaming her phone number on a live radio broadcast. And she might sound innocent and helpless, but don't test her. If you mess with my mom's pets, she will waterboard your ass with raw sewage.

I looked over at my dad, "Oh my God, she's going to get arrested again."

He sped up. "I know, I'm hurrying."

I tried dialing her, anything to get her off the radio, but she sent me to voicemail and continued ranting. Of course, that's how it always goes! The one time you *want* to talk to your mother is the moment she's too busy verbally assaulting New Jersey state troopers to take your call. After seven attempts, she answered but was still shouting at the policemen.

"Oh look, guys! My daughter's on the phone! DOES CHRIS CHRISTIE WANT TO KILL MY DAUGHTER, TOO?" Calling was clearly a mistake.

"Mom! Stop talking! We're here. Come meet me and Dad at the Sea Shell! We can get that healthy Greek salad!" We actually could not have gotten that salad, as the restaurant was closed. It didn't matter, though. She blew right past my health food distraction tactics. She sounded like she was about to start taking hostages.

"Get this! These troopers won't let us back, because Governor Chris "Cat Killer" Christie has an evacuation order in place. And it might be *two weeks* until we can go back! I'd like to see Chris Christie survive for two days without food!" Yep, hostages were definitely going to be taken, and it seemed like torture might not be off the table.

"Mom, please, come meet us now! Breathe."

In what is truly a small miracle, I convinced her to meet us in the Sea Shell's parking lot. I worried she still might decide to turn around and crash through the barricade, so I kept her on the phone.

"MOM? Stay with me. Are you driving now?"

"YES, okay!? I'm coming. Oh, hold on . . . shoot gotta go, someone's calling."

She disconnected, and I was almost certain she had a change of heart and was in the process of hanging a U-turn back to the evacuation zone. My dad pulled into the parking lot where we were supposed to meet, and as each minute passed with no sign of her battered SUV, I worried she had been taken into custody. She was not answering my calls or responding to my increasingly panicked texts. After about thirty minutes, my phone rang.

"MOM! Oh my god! Where are you!?"

"Chris Christie wants to murder my animals? Not so fast, motherfucker!" She sounded satisfied with herself.

"Where have you been?! When are you coming?"

"I'm not. I'm lying in the back of Lenny's fire truck!"

"Who the hell is Lenny?!" I could hear a muffled male voice in the background. "Kim, you're going to have to be quiet. I can hear you all the way up here, and we're getting close to the checkpoint." My mother addressed him and disconnected our call: "I'm sorry, Len! Gotta go, Spawn. I'll text you."

Via text, my mom explained that a kindhearted man named Lenny called her after hearing the impassioned radio interview. As a local firefighter, he had access to the evacuation zone and "offered" to smuggle my mother past the barricade. Now, based on past experience with my mother, I sincerely doubt this man "offered" to put his career and pension on the line for an unbalanced-sounding stranger with five dogs, two cats, and three fish. In reality, he had only "offered" to bring the animals out of the evacuation zone to my mother, or to stop by our house and feed them. Lenny's cooperation was less of an "offer" and more of a plea for mercy in the face of my mom's overwhelming powers of persuasion.

My dad's car suddenly felt like the situation room during Operation Geronimo. ObamaDad and HillaryMe were glued to the screen of my cellphone, waiting for updates from Seal Team Six. Ding! She texted me.

Holy Fireman, Kate. Couldn't say it on the phone, this man is gorgeous.

I was expecting a balding guy with a potbelly. He is GORGEOUS & he loves animals? SPERMINATOR ALERT. I'm giving him ur number.

• • • • • • • • • • • • • • • • • • • • • • • • • • • • • • • • •

My mother would find time to flirt on my behalf during a murder trial if she saw a cute lawyer with no wedding band. Why would smuggling herself past a police barricade like a human heroin balloon stop her?

• • • • • • • • • • • • • • • • • • • • • • • • • • • • • • • • •

Mother, can you just focus?

Oh, calm urself. I showed him ur picture and he thinks ur cute. His butt is like a perfect bubble bottom. I'm going to try and sneak pix for u after this.

• • • • • • • • • • • • • • • • • • • • • • • • • • • • • • • • •

"This" being a violation of a state-mandated evacuation order. Also, I bet no one on Seal Team Six paused to text Obama a booty pic on the way into Pakistan.

Omg btw, he threw this huge blue plastic tarp over me for hiding. Like the kind they wrap dead bodies in in movies. My god, this material, it's scratching up my skin! U would think they would make these things nicer.

No, no you wouldn't think that, because industrial tarps are not velour blankets.

You just said, "like the kind they wrap dead bodies in."

OMG do u think they used THIS one for that?!

Not actually, Mother!

I'm taking it off!!

MOM! DO NOT DO THAT!

Mom?

Mom!?

Mother, answer me! Did you get arrested?

**STOP TEXTING, SPAWN. LENNY YELLED AT ME. IT DINGS EVERY TIME U WRITE SOMETHING AND WE'RE AT THE BARRICADE!**

. . . . . . . . . . . . . . . . . . . . . . . . . . . . . . . . . . . .

She has never mastered the art of switching off her phone's ringer. If I decide to see a movie with my mother, put her phone on vibrate, and forget to switch it back later, I am guaranteed at least three months of complaining: "You broke my phone! Don't talk to me about buttons; it just doesn't ring anymore!!! Come home and fix it!!!"

After about twenty minutes of waiting with no updates from Seal Team Mom, I cracked. "Okay, I have to call. It's safe, right? There's no way they were at the checkpoint for this long, right?"

My dad nodded, and I dialed my mother, who answered cheerfully after the third ring. "Hello, Spawn!"

"Oh my God, you made it?"

"My God, you're such a nervous Nina! Of course we made it! I'm just pulling up to the house with Lenny; I'm going to show him more photos of you! Come in, Lenny!" For those of you who don't know, after trafficking yourself past a sea of law-enforcement officials, it is customary to invite a hot fireman to spend an evening looking at photos of your daughter.

"Anyway, we have to go, but I'm going to send Lenny out to pick up you and your father later on tonight! Here, Lenny, look at this picture of Kate. Doesn't she have a great figure?" I had resigned myself to a night of paperwork at the bail bondsman's office, so listening to her pimp me out was actually an improvement.

"No, Mother, don't. We'll just come back after the evacuation order is lifted."

"Oh really, you're going to make Dad drive all the way back to New York and climb up fourteen flights of stairs? That's crazy." Yes, *that* would be the craziest thing to happen that day.

"Mom, stop."

"Well, make sure you stop at a bathroom! Or are you exclusively pooping in trash bags now?"

Two days later, we were back home with my mother, using working toilets and playing with our menagerie of pets (that would have been absolutely fine without my mother's valiant rescue mission).*

I've always hoped that the kindhearted fireman wasn't scarred by his evening of crime with my mom. If you were and you're reading this, Lenny, let me know if you're interested in joining our little support group! A lot of people have found solace in Kim's Klub, and my mother tells me that you make a mean casserole (it's usually a potluck thing). Anyway, email me at crazy jewishmom@gmail.com.

* There is always dog food out at our house.

2:17 am

< Messages **Mother** Details

@CrazyJewishMom

Can u hear it?

What?

The sound of ur biological clock

# Rabbi Hunting

Being single sucks. Being single with Kim Friedman as your mother is a disaster. There is no one she won't give your number to. No lawyer she won't ask if he's single. No Starbucks she won't cruise for eligible men. My biological clock appears to have a direct line to her ears. It registers as a deafening alarm that won't quit blaring until she spends a few hours giving out my phone number to strangers or scheduling plastic surgery appointments with doctors who might be single. You know how dogs can register super-high-pitched sounds that humans can't hear? It's like that, except my mom hears the screams of my dying eggs as they get flushed down the toilet every month.

When I was twenty-four and single, she was convinced that my next relationship would either turn into marriage or lead down a path to barren spinsterdom. She was like a drug-sniffing police dog, trained to detect eligible "Sperminators" from a mile out. She showed my Facebook profile to strangers on the street. She loitered at the Columbia Medical School library and handed out my business cards. She catfished men by posing as me on every dating site, including the now defunct website called JMom. What's JMom, you ask? Why, it was a dating service for Jewish mothers to connect with other neurotic Jewish mothers looking to find a mate for their child.

One weekend, I invited a few friends from college to my parents' home in New Jersey, and my friend Jacob stabbed me right in the back. He broke the cardinal rule of the fellowship of children born to neurotic Jewish mothers: Never mention a wedding in the presence of a Crazy Jewish Mom, especially if her child is still single. In fairness to Jacob, my mother was interrogating him about his personal life at the time, but I still think he could have choked back some of the heartfelt delight over his sister's impending nuptials. *Thanks, Jacob.*

"Your sister's getting married! Ah, your mother must be so thrilled! How did they meet?" My mom glanced at me, the epic failure she had shot out of her own baby cannon, green with envy over this family's joy.

"Well, that's a funny story." Jacob looked over at me apologetically. His mother and mine are cut from the same cloth, so he knew exactly what was about to happen.

"The Princeton Rabbi introduced them."

I could see all the gears in my mother's brain locking into place as he said this. Ivy League. Men. Jewish. Wedding. Babies. Grandspawn. Stealing grandspawn. Grandspawn outfits. Grandspawn elementary school applications.

"THERE'S A PRINCETON RABBI?!" I worried her brain might explode from the sudden flood of dopamine. "And he does matchmaking? Kate, why didn't you tell me this?" She pounced back on Jacob before I could answer. "How did it happen? Where? When?"

Jacob explained that he became very close to Princeton's Rabbi Eitan and his wife, Gitty, while we were still in college. When his sister Joanna broke up with her boyfriend, Jacob asked the Rabbi to introduce her to someone.

I'm pretty sure my mom tuned out the rest of his words, because she was already mentally scanning the Vera Wang bridal catalogue. She had a dopey smile glued to her face, and her eyes were glazed over like she was rolling on molly. She snapped back into focus when he stopped talking.

"Can you call the Rabbi for Kate?!"

From then on, my mother's obsession with JDate and OKCupid shifted to a fixation on the Princeton Rabbi. Jacob had also mentioned that Eitan hosted alumni events in the city all the time, and she made me swear that I would go to each and every one. I attended a few of these happy hours, which were realistically just glorified singles mixers, and braced myself for the subsequent debrief with my mother every time.

When I did not immediately get married and impregnated, she decided to take control of the situation. One day after a conference call at work, I looked down at my phone to find seventeen missed calls and thirty-two text messages from my mother. This, by the way, is an entirely average number of messages to receive from her. Usually, though, this quantity comes in over the course of an afternoon, not during a quick twenty-minute meeting. I stepped outside to call her, and she answered after half a ring.

"Are you going to the alumni drinks meet-up the Rabbi is hosting tonight?"

"What? How do you know about that?"

"I found the Princeton Rabbi's Facebook page. We're friends now. Eitan. He's fabulous!" Oh no. *This is bad.*

"Mother!"

"Oh relax! He loves me, we've been chatting all day, and he wants you to come tonight!" *This is very, very bad.* "Hello!? Answer the question!"

Didn't seem like this was really a question, so much as a command. I was not planning on going. In fact, I had a glass of cabernet, some leftover Thai food, and my current boyfriend, Detective Elliot Stabler, waiting for me at home. I sighed.

"Yes, okay? Yes! I'm going."

"Good. I told him to introduce you to only the best guys. And you need to go to *all* of the parties he organizes. He told me you only go to *some* of them. He's going to tell me when you don't go, Miss 'Netflix Is My Husband' Friedman-Siegel." Oh good. The Rabbi was informing on me to my own mother.

Now that they were friends, all her Facebook stalking shifted from me to the Princeton Rabbi. I can't count the number of times she confused the search box with her status update bar and made her Facebook status: "Kim Friedman is Eitan Webb."

With unfettered access to the Rabbi's movements, my mother took full advantage. Sometimes I might have thought I was going to spend an evening tweezing ingrown pubic hairs and drinking boxed wine in bed, but I could be wrong. All depended on whether the Rabbi had posted about an event on Facebook that day. One mention of a rooftop mixer, and I'd be sipping overpriced cocktails I couldn't afford and making forced small talk with strangers for several hours. *Oh, you have four brothers? Wild! We have nothing in common, and I don't want to talk to you anymore! CAN I GO HOME AND SHAVE MY TOE HAIR NOW?!*

After a few months of these Rabbi-sponsored happy hours, my uterus remained empty, and my mom grew impatient. One evening in late November, she called me after a long day at work.

"You're still coming home for Hanukkah, right? And you're bringing your friends?"

"Yes."

"Perfect. Oooooh! I'm so excited. I have a surprise! You're not going to believe who's coming to our Hanukkah party!"

All my hair stood on end; I hadn't heard her this giddy for some time, and I tried to imagine who our mystery guest could be. Was Broadway diva Ethel Merman back from the dead and coincidentally in southern New Jersey for the holidays? Was Mick Jagger playing Hanukkah parties in an attempt to finally find his "Satisfaction"? Was Hillary Clinton getting a head start on securing the Jewish vote for her 2016 campaign? With my mom, nothing is ever really impossible.

"Who?"

"It's the Princeton Rabbi and his wife! And they're staying overnight at our house!!"

Of course they were. Keep your friends close, but keep deeply religious Jewish people who might introduce your daughter to a nice Jewish boy closer. *Clichés are clichés for a reason.* I'm very fond of Eitan and Gitty and consider them good friends, but having them sleep at our house was complicated in a way my mother failed to consider.

At this point, I think it's important to note that Rabbi Eitan Webb and his wife, Gitty—again both lovely people—are Hasidic Jews. And as Hasidic Jews, they adhere to very strict Jewish rituals—everything from dietary laws involving separate dishes for milk and meat to rigorous prayer obligations. Not to mention the fact that they cannot touch people of the opposite sex! This was especially challenging for my mother, a woman who once hugged a policeman while he was giving her a ticket.

To illustrate *my* family's level of religious observation: the last time we went to synagogue was for a Bar Mitzvah in 2002, and our bagel brunches involve serving a giant pile of bacon next to the lox and cream cheese. For those who are unfamiliar with Jewish dietary laws, pork is *the* most forbidden of all the forbidden foods.

My mother made her first Jewish mistake long before the day of the Hanukkah party: she invited them to travel to our home on a *Saturday* afternoon. Another quick Jewy primer for all you gentiles reading this: Some observant Jewish people do not use electricity or drive from Friday night at sundown until the sun sets the following day in observance of the Sabbath.

After that embarrassing faux pas, my mother decided she was going to transform herself into the Shebrew Martha Stewart and our house into a home worthy of the Jewish issue of *Architectural Digest*. On the day of the party, my mom rehearsed conversations with the Princeton Rabbi in her head and sometimes out loud a little bit too. *Oh, you have kids? How great! My daughter wants kids! But she's alone.*

She ordered a laughably enormous spread of food from Bubbie's, the only kosher restaurant in our neighborhood, hid all the bacon, and even bought six extra menorahs to hammer home what respectable Jewish people we were. And of course, she searched for the perfect, non-pork-contaminated paper dinnerware on which to serve them. All her frantic preparations that day had the kind of intensity that makes me think her internal monologue was: *If I don't choose the right paper plate design, my only daughter will die childless and be eaten by a herd of her own cats.*

We had a big boisterous group of guests at our house for the party, and she was her usual insane self for our pre-Rabbi dinner at 7 p.m., jabbering about vibrators and the transgender surgeon documentary she was working on at the time. This, of course, included an in-depth description of how plastic surgeons can invert penises and build, and I quote, "lifelike vaginas that are nicer than mine!" The Rabbi and his wife weren't scheduled to arrive until 9 p.m., because again, they are Hasidic Jewish people who observe the Sabbath and cannot drive until after sundown on Saturdays.

By 8:45, man-made vaginas were a distant memory, and my mother was visibly nervous. I even felt the need to reassure her when they were ten minutes away from our house.

"It's going to be fine. They're going to have a great time here!"

"Shoot, maybe we should have waited to eat with

them. Should I have bought new plates and silverware for them? Is paper rude?" Let me translate that: *If you die alone, it's going to be because I let the Rabbi and his wife eat off paper plates.*

"Mom, it's going to be fine. Breathe. Just remember not to get excited and hug the Rabbi."

"I FORGOT ABOUT THE HUGGING! Oh my god! This is a disaster! I was going to hug him! Why don't I just roast a pig in the middle of our living room?!"

When they arrived, my mother was uncharacteristically timid at first. She took Gitty's coat and elbowed my father until he offered to take the Rabbi's. I could see my mom silently reminding herself: *Don't hug the Rabbi. Don't hug the Rabbi. Don't hug the Rabbi.*

"It's so great to meet you in person!" She led them over to the dining room table, carefully avoiding the Rabbi's path. "I hope this is okay. We ordered you food from Bubbie's, and they promised me they have a strict kosher kitchen, and we only have paper plat—"

Gitty cut my mother off in the middle of her rambling apology. "Oh, Kim! This is perfect, thank you! This is just right."

Unfortunately, Gitty and Eitan are lovely people, and almost instantly put my mother's nerves at ease. After that and a few charming jokes from Eitan, my mother's Shebrew apron was on the floor. She instantly felt like they were family. Hell, inverted schlongs might be back on the table for discussion!

And speaking of penises, at one point she actually said, "I know you've cornered the East Coast market on Jewish manmeat, so come on??? Where's my daughter's hunky kosher strip steak?!"

All nervous pretense and niceties were gone, and she interrogated them with the sort of frankness usually reserved for the privacy of her own brain.

"Let's talk turkey here! Kate's not getting any younger; her eggs are rotting as we speak!"

If you've met my mother, you'll know that the majority of what she says out loud is pretty objectionable. Given how comfortable she felt with the Rabbi and his wife, I'm surprised she didn't scream, "BRING ME THE CIRCUMCISED SPERMINATORS, RABBI!"

Thankfully, she didn't, so Gitty and Eitan are still speaking to us. And I'm not really allowed to complain about any of it, because exactly four days after the Princeton Rabbi and his wife slept over at our house, I met my current boyfriend, Jon, at a Hanukkah party at the Princeton Club of New York. Hosted by who? Rabbi Eitan and Gitty Webb.

So, and I really can't emphasize this enough: If you force Hasidic Jewish people to sleep in your home, they might find you a hunky kosher strip steak.

11:12 pm

< Messages **Mother** Details

@CrazyJewishMom

Hey Spawn! I'm at the strip club with Jeffrey! U want to join? I'll buy u and ur boyfriend lap dances

# Buff Boys

Don't *talk to strangers.* This was my mother's mantra during my childhood, but as with everything she says, it usually had an interesting twist.

"SPAWN, DON'T TALK TO STRANGERS! Because if you do, you will get put in a dirty van with blacked-out windows and kidnapped. We *have* our own dogs, so you don't need to go chasing after a stranger with puppies or kittens. Because again, if you do, you *will* get kidnapped and never see your father or me again . . . Okay, Katie, have a good day at school!"

This led to a great deal of anxiety as a child and a lot of me shouting, "STRANGER DANGER! THAT MAN'S A PEDOPHILE!" at innocent people in parks who were just trying to walk their dogs. My mother always encouraged this behavior, smiling as I shamed upstanding orthodontists and respectable lawyers, chasing them out of Barrington Dog Park with my screams.

While she lauded *my* hostile approach to anyone unfamiliar, my mother has never, ever followed the rule "Don't talk to strangers." She talks to virtually everyone she encounters, and she has that indefinable quality, that rare sparkle, that instantly puts people at ease. Incidentally, she would make an excellent kidnapper.

You could drop her in a room filled with silent Tibetan monks, and within sixty seconds, she would have Kalsang dishing about that *fucking* Chodak, and his *bullshit need* to be at the front during morning meditation. *WE GET IT, CHODAK. YOU PRAY THE HARDEST!*

I cannot count the number of times I've gotten a text or an email or thirty voicemails raving about her new best friend whom she just accosted at Starbucks or the gym. I think the reason strangers open up to her so freely is because she is genuinely interested in hearing their stories and helping if she can. Deep down, she's a huge softy, so when she encounters someone with a broken wing, her immediate impulse is to shove them up her vaginal canal, rebirth them, and raise them properly.

My mother has high standards when it comes to bringing people into her inner circle, though. She has no interest in wasting time on someone who doesn't love her for exactly who she is. Often, she will ask a potential new friend about their thoughts on Brazilian waxing and the resemblance of sheared vaginas to the crotches of prepubescent children, just to test them. Have to make sure they're a big enough weirdo to hang with her and not run away at the first whisper of pubic hair. And using this technique, my mom has amassed a collection of fascinating strangers who have become her nearest and dearest friends.

One of her most interesting companions is a Jewish gay male strip club entrepreneur named Jeffrey. My mother and I met Jeffrey at a casting call for *Gay Jersey Shore*. His life story is fascinating: Jeff grew up destitute in Brooklyn, dropped out of middle school, and became one of the biggest drug dealers in the Tri-State area in order to take care of his family. Some of the anecdotes from his life as a gay Jewish teenage drug dealer are unreal—he even went to jail, but that's a whole other book,* and he has long since turned his life around. The moment my mother and Jeffrey bonded, male strippers became a part of my daily reality.

"Oh, you're going to have dinner with your boyfriend and his parents? I want to come! And I want them to meet Jeffrey too."

"You're going out tonight? You and your friends should stop by Jeffrey's strip club in Midtown; I'll tell him to reserve a table!"

"Jeffrey and his husband are coming to stay at our house for the weekend, and I'm giving them your bedroom. Has the best view, and Lord knows my own daughter never comes to visit me!"

When I moved into my Brooklyn apartment that she so lovingly named "The Deathtrap," my mother naturally turned to Jeffrey in my hour of need. I'll acknowledge the apartment could be nicer. For instance, it would be cool if the building weren't slanted to the point that a lemon resting on the kitchen counter rolls

* A book Jeffrey has written and is self-publishing! Seriously, check it out: *Braverman* by Jeffrey Wachman.

to the floor. But alas, I'm on a budget, a budget that doesn't allow for fancy apartments, let alone expensive moving companies. It is also located on the fourth floor of a walk-up apartment building, and my mother had asked Jeffrey to help me move my stuff up the four flights of stairs. Jeffrey really loves my mother.

When the buzzer rang, my boyfriend Jon and I climbed down the rickety steps of my new building to meet them. As soon as we opened the door, we came face-to-face with Jeffrey and my mother, leaning against a huge BuffBoyzz-branded SUV. The car was set up as a mobile billboard for his strip club: advertising prom-

inently displayed nude asses and barely concealed penises all over the car.

One of my new neighbors walked past the van and into the building to get her mail as Jeffrey barreled toward me, bodybuilder arms open wide in a skimpy white tank top.

"Kate, it's so good to see you!" He hugged me and turned to Jon. "And you must be Superjew! Heard so much about you! I'm Jeffrey!" My mother had lovingly nicknamed my boyfriend "Superjew" when we started dating, because after my train wreck of an ex, a nice Jewish boy felt a lot like a hero.

"Nice to meet you, Jeffrey. You can call me Jon." He extended a hand and smiled politely. Jeffrey ignored the handshake and pulled Jon into a bear hug against his tattooed torso, shouting over his shoulder toward my mother.

"Kim, you didn't tell me what a little hottie the boyfriend was! Guess that's what the *super* in Superjew is all about! Good work, Kate."

"Do you see this dump, Jeffrey?" My mother folded

her arms and strolled over. "Look at the fire escape—they should just hang a sign: Rapists and Robbers Welcome!" She turned to me. "So, Kate, did you thank Jeffrey for pitching in?"

"Well, I was just about to! Seriously, Jeffrey, thank you *so* much for doing this. This is really incredibly nice."

"Listen, it's nothing. For this woman, I'd do anything!" He waved me off and jovially threw an arm around my mother.

We spent the next hour running up and down the steps, shuttling my new belongings from the strip-club-branded SUV to my apartment. People walking by on the street whipped their heads toward our X-rated spectacle, but I was more focused on the conversation Jeffrey was having with my boyfriend.

A bit of context: After five years in prison, Jeffrey, ever the entrepreneur, started building a brand-new *legal* stripper-based empire from scratch and completely turned his life around. Now he wants to expand that empire to the Internet.

"So, Jon, Kim told me you make phone apps."

My boyfriend nodded politely. "Well, yes, I'm a developer, but I don't typically work on that kind of thing."

"But you *can* make apps?"

"Well, I guess I cou—"

"Oh, Jon, you must talk to Jeffrey about this." My mother interrupted him. "I think it's an absolutely fabulous app idea. You know, it's important to do these things while you're young. Before you start a family."

Jeffrey went ahead with his pitch as we carried furniture up the very public, paper-thin-walled staircase of my building.

"So, you know how you sometimes want to hire a private dancer? And you have no idea where the closest one is to you?"

"Uh, sure." Jon glanced at me as he answered. *No.* No, he did not. My boyfriend is possibly the most buttoned-up, straitlaced man in the United States. I don't think he's even met a person who has hired a private dancer. Well, except for my mother, of course.

"So, what I want to do is make an app where everyday people can find and chat with the closest stripper.

And on the app they can figure out rates and shit and then hire them."

"I think it's fabulous, and Jeffrey knows everything there is to know about this business. He thinks it's going to be a hit!" My mother smiled proudly. "Jon, you're this big computer guy . . . *what's the holdup?*"

"Aww, thanks, Kim!" Jeffrey turned back to Jon, after setting down a table in my apartment. "What do you think, Jon? Would you want to make the app? We could go in fifty-fifty. We could be partners on it!"

I glared at my mother and she shrugged at me, shaking her head. "What? I think it's fabulous. Could make a lot of money! Sex sells, Kate. You and Jon need to wake up and smell the G-strings!"

After what felt like hours of moving and listening to my mother complain about Brooklyn hipsters, mason jars, and my dwindling egg supply, my thrift shop furniture had been transferred from the stripper mobile to my apartment. Jeffrey had to leave for a BuffBoyzz club night he was hosting that evening, so my mother and I halted our Clorox Wipe frenzy to say good-bye.

"Jeffrey, thank you so much, really. So sweet of you to do this." I hugged him.

"Of course. Any time! And I'm telling you, when you finish tonight, come by the club. I'll take care of you guys."

"I'll try, Jeffrey." My mom kissed him on the cheek. "Just have to convince these two boring millennials to come out. Hopefully it's a bachelorette party. Maybe that'll give Superjew here some inspiration to propose to my daughter!" She looked pointedly at Jon, but he just smiled and got up to say good-bye. When asked about my mom's outrageous antics and aggressive proposal talk directly, Jon always shrugs and says something to the effect of, "Listen, she just says what a lot of moms think but don't actually say out loud. At least she's up front about it."* Jon walked Jeffrey to the door.

"Let me know if you want to do the stripper app. Could be really good. I'm telling you, it'll be huge." He hugged my boyfriend.

* I'm not sure most moms even think it's a good idea to ask their daughter's boyfriend to go to a gay male strip club or build a DIY pole-dancing app. So Jon is truly a good sport.

"Definitely." Jon patted him on the back, and Jeffrey released him but then grasped his shoulder, making deliberate eye contact.

"Listen, you treat her right. Got it?"

Because if my mother isn't a terrifying enough specter to ward off men who might be interested in dating me, now you also run the risk of incurring the wrath of my "Uncle Jeff," a formerly incarcerated bodybuilding hunk who can be called upon at any moment to come and beat the shit out of you with a posse of ripped gay male strippers.

7:11 am

< Messages **Mother** Details

@CrazyJewishMom

What're u working on today, spawn?

Writing this AM and then I have a couple meetings with publishers to pitch my idea. I'm really nervous.

Don't be nervous. Ur a great writer and u light up any room u go into

But wear bright lipstick. And for the love of God, put on ur SPANX

Hot today, so bring a hair iron in case of Jewfro. Also put bronzing lotion on ur legs. No offense but looking at them is like looking directly into the sun. "Blinded by the light" more like "BLINDED BY KATE'S CALVES."

# #CrazyJewishMom

When my Instagram account went viral, it felt surreal. I started getting emails from book publishers, and I was excited, but when I began receiving messages from shows like *Steve Harvey* and *Dr. Phil,* I couldn't believe it. *My* mother? On television? I wanted to throw up.

When *Nightline* emailed, I actually thought it was a joke. They want *us* to come on their Peabody Award–winning, investigative journalism show? *Don't they realize my mother will almost certainly sexually harass Dan Harris? America's beloved anchor!*

Of course, my mom was up for absolutely anything. I never worry about her being shy. I worry about whether or not she'll try to pimp me out on live TV: *She wouldn't ask that respected ABC* Nightline *anchor if he's single? She did! She wouldn't try to talk about her vagina on live Canadian television? She would! She couldn't possibly ask Steve Harvey to do Kegels with her on the set of his nationally syndicated talk show?! She did!* I truly never thought I'd see my mother encourage Steve Harvey to fire imaginary Kegel balls out of his fictional vagina like a cannon.

Being on this weird Internet journey with my mom has been fairly amusing, as she might be the least technologically inclined human being on the planet. Seriously, she still uses an AOL email address and calls me every time she wants to record an episode of *Scandal*. The experience has also been inspiring for me—for the last year, I've watched my mom unapologetically and fearlessly (let me) expose her life and opinions to hundreds of thousands of people every day. And her confidence gave me the kick in the pants I needed during one of the most nerve-wracking moments of my life:

In the spring of 2014, I decided to quit my job. This might not sound terribly scary, but I'm someone who doesn't love change. For instance, one of the central criteria I used for choosing my current apartment was that it needed to fall inside the delivery range of the

Thai restaurant I order from four nights a week. Rental apartments change, but competitively priced Thai food is forever. I *do* love financial security and job stability, and these are not things that come with the decision to leave a corporate job with luxuries like dental plans, 401(K)s, and paychecks.

I have always dreamed about a career in writing, and because of the success of my Instagram account, I was lucky enough to have a promising opportunity to do that. But it was just that, "a promising opportunity"—not a signed contract, not even a freelance offer, it was a chance to *maybe* write a book about all the crazy antics my mother and I have gotten into over the years if, and only if, I could put together a decent book proposal.

I was working a high-stress, (more than) full-time job all day, and running four Instagram accounts at night (which is a fair amount of work in itself) and trying to write a coherent book proposal between the hours of midnight and 7 a.m. There's a certain kind of delirious exhaustion a human body can reach where a person fails to notice that they've started urinating with the toilet lid down. How do I know that? Because I peed all over a perfectly good pair of Hanky-Pankys before work one day. I didn't think adult diapers would go over well at the office, so I knew it was time to make a decision. I also fully recognize that this is the epitome of a first-world problem—*should I quit my day job and focus on my writing?* To even be able to ask that question is a fortunate position to be in, no matter how much urine is spilled or how many panties may be ruined in the process.

So, I ovaried up, channeled my mother, and slammed my security badge on my boss's desk shouting, "I QUIT! IT'S TIME FOR ME TO SPREAD MY WINGS AND SHARE *MY* VAGINA MONOLOGUE WITH THE WORLD, SUCKAS!!"

No, none of that happened. But on the day I officially put in my notice, I knew my mother would be proud of my decision to strike out on my own and go after my dream.

That evening, I ordered an Uber on the company

card for the last time and pulled off my workplace control tops in the backseat. I texted my mom from the Brooklyn Bridge, a little anxious but mostly excited to tell her the news. I wanted to thank her, because she was the reason I had the courage to take this risk:

. . . . . . . . . . . . . . . . . . . . . . . . . . . . . . . . . . .

Mom ok, I've been looking for the right way to tell you this for a bit now, and a text probably isn't ideal, but I articulate myself best when I'm writing, so . . .

**U finally dumped Superjew?? PLEASE**

No haha I left my job.

**Omg u got fired? What happened?**

No no no . . . I quit. I want to focus full time on writing. I'm still young, and it's now or never, no kids, etc. Jon agrees.

**Oh, well if the guy who refuses to marry u agrees . . . then by all means!!!!!**

**Kate, wake up and smell the dog poop outside ur front door. This is not an episode of GIRLS. This is ur life. SINGLE, DEATHTRAP APARTMENT, MASON JARS, and now UR UNEMPLOYED?**

**CALL ME IMMEDIATELY!!**

• • • • • • • • • • • • • • • • • • • • • • • • • • • • • • • • • • •

Not exactly how I hoped the conversation would go. I didn't even have a chance to call her, because my phone began ringing.

"I can't talk now, Kate!" *You called to tell me you can't talk?* "Your father and I are painting the basement for when you have to move back home, you MILLENNIAL!!!!!"

"Mom, just listen."

"I'm sorry, I can't hear you over the sound of your rent checks bouncing!"

"MOM! You're the one who always tells me I should be writing! This is my chance to go for it!"

"Yeah, go for it, but with health insurance and a gym membership!"

I imagined what my mother would do if she were in my situation. Would the woman who moved out to LA at twenty-six without a driver's license, a job, or a place to live in order to pursue her dream of becoming a TV director/porn writer give up now? Would she hijack this Uber and speed to her boss's office, begging for her job back? No, she'd believe in herself and freeball it over the bridge to her new adventure. Unemployment, here I come!

By the time I got back to Brooklyn, my mom was on board too, singing, "I am woman, hear me roar!" She texted me:

**Spawn, I can't believe u didn't tell me. But ok go for it! But u better win the Pulitzer. No sex 50 shades stuff.**

**And don't write in some STUPID ARTISANAL BRKLYN COFFEE SHOP!**

hahah ok I promise no coffee shops.

This turned out to be a lie, as I wrote a lot of this book sipping cold brew iced coffee in a Brooklyn shop just *bursting* with man buns.

. . . . . . . . . . . . . . . . . . . . . . . . . . . . . . . . . . . . . . .

**And don't worry about paying the rent. I know Jeff will get u a job bartending at BuffBoyzz at night.**

NO do not do that! I don't know how to make drinks, and Buff Boys is a gay strip club!! No one wants to see me.

**Oh please. 1. Ur a Pton Grad. U can learn to mix drinks. 2. Gay club, straight club . . . No one cares anymore. Didn't u read Caitlyn's interview? LABELS R OUT. So 1999.**

**Hashtag##No1CaresWhatsInUrCrotch##**

. . . . . . . . . . . . . . . . . . . . . . . . . . . . . . . . . . . . . . .

Yes, this is how my mother thinks hashtags work, and I pray that no one ever corrects her.

In retrospect, I'm not sure what the hell I was thinking. I had a modicum of Internet notoriety and a dream to be sure, but also no idea how I was going to pay my rent that month. So, we'll see how this next chapter of my life goes, but I know that if I am even a tiny fraction of the fearless, badass person my mother is, I'll be okay. And besides, if things ever get really rough, I can always follow in my mom's footsteps and write porn.

# Acknowledgments

I would like to thank: My followers on social media—truly, you were wonderful and kind throughout this process. There were at least a dozen occasions on which a lovely comment or message from you made me feel like less of a human pile of garbage (and by the end of writing this, I hadn't showered for five consecutive days, so that's something!).

Julia Weigel . . . oh my, I definitely cannot express my thanks and love for you in a single sentence, so I'll just say: "Who cares? Live ya life!" Moira Weigel for being one of the only forces keeping me sane while I wrote this book. Actually, the entire Weigel clan: Kathy and Bill Weigel for years of kindness and for putting a roof over my head on more than one occasion of homelessness. Also, Jack Altman for having a truly enormous face.

Jacob Loewenstein, Yael Nachajon, Ben Weisman, and Joanna Loewenstein for being *okay* people and for letting me write about them by name! Kham Kidia for agreeing (in advance of receiving his MD) to perform all my mother's future Botox injections. Jon Miller for being a boss and for loving Kathy Griffin's early 2000's Bravo series, *My Life on the D-List,* as much as I do. Sophie Greenberg (and Julia again) for answering hundreds of disgusting questions about STDs. Jed Weintrob for protecting me from electromagnetic radiation.

Morgan Shanahan for igniting this whole adventure. Tony Etz, Darren Trattner, Rachel Adler, and Olivia Blaustein for responding to emails far earlier than any of them should have been awake. Mary Wyatt for saving the day. Robert Profusek and Mary Kosearas for listening to my angst. Cait Hoyt for her support and guidance (and for listening to my angst). Suzanne O'Neill for making me a better writer and Trish Boczkowski for carrying the torch to the finish line (and letting me camp out in her office for forty-eight deeply neurotic hours). Jenni Zellner and Jesse Aylen for keeping the wheels on this process.

Zachary Glass for tolerating multiple forced readings of half-baked chapters. Team Kegels for everything. My entire family for being supportive of my hibernation and understanding my absence at holidays while I wrote this thing. All United States law enforcement agencies for not pressing charges against my mother (please)!

Jonathan Bradford Glass for being a truly enormous Matzoh Ball and for tolerating me (and my mother). Also, I'm sorry for revealing your ridiculous middle name. Moo.

And my mom and dad for more than I could possibly articulate in the last line of a book that in all likelihood no one is even reading. I imagine you (the reader) closed the book after the last page (if not after the cat-stealing chapter), and thought, "Huh, I probably should have bought *The Girl on the Train* instead." But if you *are* reading this: (1) Thank you. (2) Know that my mother and father are two of the best human beings in the universe, and I love them with all my heart. I hit the genetic jackpot getting them as parents, and I feel like the luckiest human to have been raised by them. Also, to not have been dropped on my head as a child . . . my mother has exceedingly poor spatial reasoning skills.

# Credits

Illustrations by guteksk7/Shutterstock

Photo on page 16: Mary Wyatt

Photo on page 63: Craig Amerkhanian

Photo on page 76: Jackie Bello

Photo on page 233: Jeffrey Wachman

Photo on page 250: Lauren O'Jea

All other photos courtesy of the author

# About the Author

KATE SIEGEL is a writer and a social media guru who started the hit Instagram account @CrazyJewishMom. She has been featured on *BuzzFeed*, *Elite Daily*, *The Huffington Post*, *Cosmo*, Today.com, Vogue.com, in *People* magazine, and on *Nightline* and *The Ellen DeGeneres Show*. She previously served as an associate producer for Condé Nast Entertainment, overseeing digital video for *Teen Vogue*, *Bon Appétit*, *The New Yorker* Festival, *Condé Nast Traveler*, and *Self*. Prior to joining Condé Nast, Kate studied English, creative writing, and theater at Princeton University. Her one-act play *Sam the Man* was a winner of the Sondheim Young Playwright's Inc. National Playwriting Competition and was produced at their annual New York showcase. The play was also selected by the Blank Theatre Young Playwrights Festival and received a full production at the Egyptian Theatre in Hollywood.